Wicked CARLISLE

The Dark Side of the Cumberland Valley

Joseph David Cress

THE
History
PRESS

Published by The History Press
Charleston, SC 29403
www.historypress.net

All images courtesy of the Cumberland County Historical Society unless otherwise noted.

First published 2012

Manufactured in the United States

ISBN 978.1.60949.525.1

Library of Congress CIP data applied for.

Contents

Acknowledgements

Thanks to my wife, Stacey, for her love and support as I work to establish myself as an author. You've always been my chief inspiration.

I also extend my gratitude to friends and family, especially two men who had a profound impact on my life. My father, Paul Robert Cress, has always been there—quietly proud and supportive of my work. From you, I learned how to be patient and calm under pressure and just how important it is to contribute and give something back to society (despite all my clutter). Then there is Tim Wolfe, who has been like a younger brother. You taught me the freedom of creativity and how inspiring it can be just to brainstorm and dream big. I will always remember the wicked fun we've had over the course of our friendship.

I also want to thank the professional and helpful staff at the Cumberland County Historical Society where most of the research for this book took place. From the start, I've been impressed by the quantity and quality of information stored at your facility. I especially want to thank photo archivist Richard Tritt and his crew for their work in helping me select and process the majority of the images found throughout this book.

Lastly, my gratitude goes out to the hardworking and dedicated staff at the *Sentinel* newspaper in Carlisle. Every day, you defy the odds, overcome obstacles and strive to put out a quality product. My years spent in that newsroom have prepared me to fulfill my dream of being an author.

Introduction

T he best villains are drawn in shades of gray. Rarely in life or in literature are characters totally good or evil, black or white. Humanity has always been this ball of conflicting and complex emotions. The villains with the most impact are often cut from the same crude fabric as the heroes, even though their cloth may be a bit more frayed along the edges.

So often we are drawn to the exploits of those who are not just noteworthy but also nefarious. We may condemn their actions in public but envy them in secret for their boldness. Let's be honest: The wicked fascinate us. For proof, you need only look at online statistics that show how crime reports consistently get the most hits on newspaper websites. This book is about villains, the wicked folk who once walked the streets of old Carlisle and now form as much of its history as the heroes.

Early on, Carlisle was a rough-and-tumble town on the very edge of civilization. Its streets bore witness to riots and jailbreaks, frontier expeditions and an enemy invasion. Even today, this town in south central Pennsylvania is at a crossroads as a strategic transportation hub nestled in the heart of the Cumberland Valley. Yet within this heart, there beats the pulse of individuals as complex as anyone else and as prone to vice as they are virtue.

In the pages that follow, you will meet a rowdy drunk, pesky "firebugs," a disturbed cross-dresser, an unfortunate namesake and a mother-daughter team of flesh peddlers. You will trace the footsteps of an arson ring, witness horrific explosions, visit a notorious whorehouse and attend a bizarre funeral with two rival widows. You will be privy to campus capers, trade school injustice, secret conspiracies and early American crime syndicates. For a time, you will embrace the wicked and welcome them into your home.

Staff of the *Daily Sentinel* newspaper, circa 1884.

My hope is that this book sheds light on shady characters while revealing something of their humanity to the reader.

There are thirteen stories of trauma and temptation, trickery and tantrums spanning almost two hundred years of Carlisle history, from the Revolutionary War to the early 1970s. As much as possible, I have used primary sources to tell each story from the individual's point of view. I have found that history is far more engaging when told through the eyes of those who lived it. Studying our past is not supposed to be tedious. I see history as a pathway to a better understanding of our present day and as a wellspring from which to draw lessons as we venture into the future.

Much of what follows is based on firsthand accounts by fellow journalists—many of whom had their names lost to history before bylines were a common newsroom practice. This book is my tribute to their hard work and dedication in bringing to us history in its first draft. This book is for them to show the public there is still value in newspapers even as the industry struggles to stay relevant and competitive in a noisy world crowded with demands for our attention.

So welcome now to the vile side of Carlisle. Brace yourself going forward. Be sure to buckle up. You're in for one hell of a ride.

Part I

Frontier Felons

There is no honor among thieves." This old saying rings true today as it has for more than two centuries, since the United States was a struggling young upstart of a nation. *Wicked Carlisle* begins with the story of a veteran whose guilt by association left him hanging by a noose as just another casualty in a war of economics that used funny money as ammunition. We then turn to a man-made history—part fact, part folklore—formed by criminal exploits that defied limits and social conventions. Lewis the Robber lives on as a legend—a chivalrous rogue who stole both hearts and treasure until he himself became the willing pawn in a dirty game of politics that used his reputation as a weapon.

Temple of Fame

The Plight of Christopher Shockey

C hristopher Shockey may have suspected he had purchased a death sentence for himself during his spending spree in Carlisle. He was long gone by the time the local vendors realized he had passed them counterfeit money. For five months, the veteran soldier evaded capture until his arrest on South Mountain in September 1779. While an inmate in Cumberland County Jail, he pleaded his case to authorities until the hangman came to collect on a life tainted by his family's bad reputation.

In February 1779, Christopher Shockey was discharged from the Continental army after serving three years with the Seventh Pennsylvania Regiment. There is speculation that after all the sacrifice of military life, he wanted to treat himself to a good time, so Shockey asked his brothers if he could borrow the counterfeit money or purchase it at less than its face value.

Shockey arrived in Carlisle sometime in the afternoon or evening of April 23, 1779. He visited three vendors including Michael Miller, who owned a clothing store on the east side of Hanover Street two doors north of Louther Street. There he bought new clothes before walking around the corner and almost two blocks east to the barbershop of Joseph Sabole, located midway between Bedford and East Streets on the south side of Louther Street. There, he paid for a bath, shave and haircut. Looking all dapper, Christopher Shockey then made his way to a tavern kept by William Holmes, just east of St. John's Episcopal Church on the town square.

By the next morning when all three vendors complained to county sheriff James Johnston that they had been paid with counterfeit money, Shockey

This detail of an early plan of Carlisle, drawn by John Creigh in 1764, shows the public square and the surrounding block where Christopher Shockey went on his shopping spree with counterfeit money.

had disappeared. Authorities issued an arrest warrant for the fugitive, whose older brother Valentine (seventeen years Shockey's senior) was a leader in a gang of counterfeiters, highwaymen and horse thieves. These men operated as part of a late eighteenth-century crime syndicate that extended from Virginia, north to Canada and included southern Pennsylvania and the Cumberland Valley. They intimidated the population by burning the property of anyone who spoke out or moved against them. Brazen, these criminals flaunted their wealth by riding the best horses and by wearing the finest clothes and jewelry.

This gang eluded justice until Michael Milligan, an engraver from Black's Gap, Blair County, pled guilty to a misdemeanor charge of possessing metal plates used to make counterfeit money. In exchange for leniency, Milligan agreed to inform on the syndicate. In a deposition taken on September 10, 1779, he testified that Isaac and Abraham Shockey came to his home in 1776 and paid him to make plates for fake thirty-dollar bills. The following year, he was asked by Joseph Nicholson and John King to engrave two more plates—one for five-dollar bills and one for seven-dollar bills. Shortly thereafter, Valentine Shockey asked Milligan to make plates for counterfeit thirty-dollar bills. This was followed by a request from Isaac and Abraham in late April 1779 to make plates for forty-dollar bills.

Authorities used this information to launch a manhunt and nab Christopher Shockey. Although Milligan did not mention him by name, Christopher was probably implicated because of the close association with his brothers and because he was a fugitive from justice. Meanwhile, Milligan was sentenced to stand in the pillory in York for an hour on November 8, 1779, before being confined in York County Jail until July 4, 1780.

Searching for the counterfeiters was not easy because they used the long, narrow valleys of the Blue Mountains as a covert travel route and its secluded coves as hideouts. Christopher Shockey was apprehended by a posse under the command of Johnston and Squire John Bournes, a magistrate of what was then Antrim Township in Cumberland County, now Washington Township in Franklin County. Posse members had set up an all-night vigil after surrounding the suspected hideout of the counterfeiters.

Sometime during the night, a footman wearing a military hat came through the picket line and was mistaken at first for a posse member. When the man was finally challenged, he failed to give the proper countersign and fled into the wilderness. The pursuit continued until he was surrounded by posse members and detained at the point of Bournes's bayonet. Identified as Christopher Shockey, the man was marched off the mountain and then transported to Cumberland County Jail in Carlisle. The court denied the young Shockey bail, and the grand jury indicted him on October 18, 1779, on charges of counterfeiting and passing bogus thirty-dollar bills similar to those issued by the Continental Congress on July 22, 1776.

On October 20, 1779, Christopher Shockey was put on trial, and the jury heard testimony from the three victims of his April 23, 1779 shopping spree in downtown Carlisle. The panel found Shockey not guilty of the counterfeiting charge but guilty of passing bogus money. The judge sentenced him to be hanged, and on November 23, 1779, the State of Pennsylvania issued a warrant for execution, setting the date as December 11, 1779. But before this could happen, Joseph Reed, president of the Supreme Executive Council, heard petitions from Carlisle-area residents who begged for leniency.

Pleas for mercy on his behalf focused on young Shockey's military service along with the helpless state of his wife and three small children. Given the reputation of his family name, none of this carried any weight for the condemned man. Charles Lukas, an acting colonel at Carlisle Barracks, said he knew Shockey as a good and faithful soldier in the Seventh Pennsylvania Regiment. However, Lukas only took command of the unit after Colonel Thomas Hartley resigned in early 1779, so Shockey never served directly under Lukas. This unit saw action at the Battles of Paoli, Brandywine and Germantown under the command of Hartley.

Jailer Matthew Atkinson wrote how Christopher Shockey behaved himself while a prisoner in Carlisle. Neighbors who had past dealings with Shockey testified how they never knew him to pass any counterfeit money. They lived in what is today Franklin and Hamilton Townships in Franklin County. In seeking a pardon, Shockey asked authorities to consider his willingness to serve again in the military. "Your petitioner...most earnestly solicits and pleads for your honor's clemency and mercy," the condemned man wrote before signing his letter "Christopher Shockey—unhappy brother in the Temple of Fame." In his paper, "Colonial Counterfeiters of the Blue Ridge," John H. McClellan said the temple of fame reference was probably Shockey's way of saying the reputation of his family name had earned him the death penalty. The pleas of mercy failed, and Shockey was executed on schedule.

As for Valentine, he eluded capture and continued his life of crime through the late eighteenth century. Authorities believed the gang operated out of a cave east of the Great Falls on Falls Creek. A posse in pursuit of Valentine once torched his house hoping the fire would draw out the counterfeiter into an ambush, but this failed when Valentine refused to budge from his lair and decided instead to let his property burn. There was a reason why authorities resorted to such extreme measures to combat counterfeiting: It had become a matter of economic survival for the fledgling nation.

The start of the American Revolution saw a Continental Congress unable to pay for an army, and the bureaucracy needed to run a centralized national government. Although the states collected taxes, that money was used to support their own governments. As a result, Congress issued $240 million

Colonial money from the Cumberland County Historical Society collection.

worth of paper money during the war that had no financial backing other than the promise by the United States to redeem these bills of credit with gold or silver sometime in the future. Despite protests from Congress, the states printed another $200 million of their own paper money.

Quick to see the weakness of such a system, the British flooded the market with counterfeit bills hoping to destroy the American economy. They did this by shipping printing presses and false currency through blockaded ports. While the colonies used set type to print paper money, the British used engraved plates to make higher-quality fakes that looked more genuine than the real thing. As more money was distributed, its value depreciated, even though Congress enacted laws to control prices and to punish those who refused to accept Continental money at its face value. Such laws could not be enforced, and the currency continued to depreciate at an alarming rate until it became worthless. The result was runaway inflation, a prosperous black market and financial ruin for hundreds of American families.

Counterfeiting and passing counterfeit bills became crimes equivalent to treason during the Revolutionary War. Conditions only worsened until the currency failed entirely in 1781. Robert Morris of Philadelphia organized the Bank of North America to stabilize the economy by taking in money from prominent families loyal to the cause and loans from such friendly nations as France and Holland. This bank was also supported by states putting up provisions like flour, tobacco, rice and other goods that were then sold as commodities to the West Indies for gold or silver. Still, counterfeit money served the British as a highly effective weapon of war.

In his deposition, Milligan also mentioned James Nugent of Cumberland County as someone who passed counterfeit money. Like the Shockeys, the Nugent brothers were reputed criminals. In July 1760, Thomas Nugent was arraigned on theft charges and later convicted. His sentence included fifteen lashes on the public whipping post and a fine of fifty pounds. In court again, just months later, Thomas Nugent told the judge he could not pay his fine and requested that he be sold off as an indentured servant for seven years. In 1779, two of the Nugent brothers were called three times to appear in court but failed to answer the summons. James was charged with passing counterfeit money while Benjamin was wanted for arson. The law would eventually catch up with them.

The story goes that James and Benjamin encountered a man one day on the road near Chambersburg. Thinking that the bottle the man carried contained whiskey, they demanded that he turn it over to them. The man gave it up without a struggle. When one of the brothers took a swig from the bottle, they found out that it contained yeast, so they broke the bottle over the traveler's head and proceeded to beat him up. The brothers were later arrested and tried in Carlisle on May 22, 1780, for highway robbery. They were convicted and sentenced to death by hanging on June 17, 1780. It is said that on the day of their execution, the brothers refused to leave their jail cell, prompting the authorities to smoke them out by burning sulfur under their cell door. As they left, one brother remarked to the other, "Hell can be no worse than that."

Aside from counterfeiters, bands of horse thieves profited from selling animals stolen from farms to British forces occupying Philadelphia. Though the thieves preyed mostly upon settlers in the eastern counties of Pennsylvania, there were times when they operated in Cumberland County. It is believed some of these criminals were members of the county militia. After they could no longer sell to the British, the thieves stole animals from Pennsylvania farms to transport over state lines and resell in other states where they were not recognized by lawmen.

My Manifold Crimes

Lewis the Robber

When you drink from the well of regret, there can never be enough cool liquid to quench the fire of a troubled heart. Carlisle had given birth to a villain, but deep down, David Lewis wanted out of the criminal lifestyle that had turned him into a fugitive counterfeiter and robber. At that moment, he needed to quell his thirst with water drawn from a street pump into the cup of his hands, but instead of relief, the pain of all his bad choices came flowing back.

He had arrived in Carlisle around twilight one evening disguised as a cripple. A piece of green silk covered one eye, and there was a large black patch on his left cheek. For a time, he wandered aimlessly from place to place carrying a bundle of old clothing beneath one arm. "Anxious to avoid the risk of attention, I changed my situation frequently and mixed with different companies," Lewis recalled in a jail confession made on the eve of his death. "I became a party to…conversations carried on and … acquainted with the passing transactions of the times."

His plan was to visit his mother in Bellefonte to arrange for the safe passage of his wife and children to Canada where Lewis intended to retire into relative obscurity. But first, the Robin Hood of Pennsylvania had to visit his birthplace and, more specifically, the home along South Hanover Street where he was born on March 4, 1790, and where he spent the first three years of his life. Childhood memories drove Lewis to stoop down and kiss the doorsill where he used to sit with his mother as they watched the older boys play out in the street. Overcome with nostalgia, he walked a short distance to the site of an old well where he found the street pump. What he felt at that moment was documented in his confession:

The comparison between what I had been and what [I] am now...filled my heart with anguish...I felt as one possessed of two distinct souls...One inclining him to virtue, and the other drawing him to vice...The strength of the latter prevailed over the weakness of the former, and plunged me in that deep and black abyss of guilt for which I found it impossible to rise. My heart was torn to pieces by the violence of feelings which now agitated me...I shed a profuse shower of tears; but tears afford relief only to those who are at peace with themselves...This gentle fluid of humanity, which ran from my enflamed eyes, only scalded my cheeks without relieving my bursting heart. I remain for some time in this agony of feeling, transfixed to the spot like a statue of despair.

This old town pump used to stand on the north side of the first block of West Pomfret Street.

Lewis might have stayed there for some time had it not been for the sound of music, which drew him up a nearby alley to a stone house where he stopped to listen. The melody sounded familiar, almost like church music. He opened the gate, went up to a window and peeked through a broken shutter. There, an elderly couple was closing their day with hymns sung in worship. Lewis was so moved by what he witnessed that he let out an enthusiastic "Amen!" just as the couple concluded a prayer. He fled back into the night undetected.

On reaching a safe distance, Lewis stopped to reflect on what had just happened. He recalled how he felt after hearing a sermon by a reverend bishop in New York City earlier in his nefarious career. It made Lewis sad just thinking how easy it was for him to disregard all religious talk and moral teachings as he indulged in "guilty pleasures and criminal scenes." He was known, far and wide, as Lewis the Robber, and yet he saw himself more as an equalizer who took money from wealthy merchants, landowners and tax collectors to help poor families and laborers facing foreclosure or bankruptcy. His criminal activity spanned some twenty years and ranged throughout Pennsylvania and into New York, New England and Canada.

The night of his visit, Lewis walked the streets of Carlisle in search of a place to rest. With all this regret over past sins, he was tired and needed sleep for the next day's journey to East Pennsboro Township, where he planned to meet up with his gang members. "I happened to pass by the public offices," Lewis said in his confession. Perhaps he was referring to the original town hall and Cumberland County courthouse that stood on the square until 1845, when both were destroyed by arson. Finding an open door, he went inside and used his bundle of old clothes as a pillow. Lewis slept soundly on the hard floor until he was awakened by someone crying out in the night. He described what happened next:

> I was not long in discovery…the sound came from a poor unfortunate maniac of the name of Baggs, who I had often seen in Carlisle and in other places. I accosted him without apology saying "George, be still." The inoffensive idiot immediately replied "Oh yes, Bill" and without much more adieu retired to a corner of the entry, where he laid down and remained quiet until he fell asleep…much happier than hundreds who lie in beds of down under canopies of velvet.

The next morning, Lewis was gone, and within months of that final visit, he was in a jail cell in Bellefonte dying of gangrene from a gunshot wound that shattered his right shoulder and arm. He had refused to let a doctor amputate the limb but instead made his confession to the world. In it, Lewis explained how his parents were poor and had to work long hours for the family to survive. As such, they had little time left over to pay close attention to their children.

"I grew up," Lewis recalled, "as most boys in such situations do—without regard for men and little fear of God." In 1793, his family moved from Carlisle to Bellefonte so his father could take the job of deputy surveyor of what was then Northumberland County. Lewis did not specify what misfortunes his father encountered "rising out of this official conduct," only that the situation had "little mended for the better" by the time his father died in 1796. His death left the family ill-prepared for the future.

With little education, Lewis stayed with his mother working odd hours on nearby farms until 1807, when he left home and joined the army. While Lewis enjoyed the camaraderie of military service, his restless spirit rebelled at its strict discipline. He deserted after a sergeant charged him with a petty offense. Drawn by the money offered to recruits, David Lewis later reenlisted under the alias Armstrong Lewis. When the army learned of his prior service and desertion, he was arrested and confined to the stockade at Carlisle Barracks pending a court-martial. He was later found guilty and sentenced to death. In desperation, the condemned man thought of his mother:

> *It pained me to the soul to think that the ignoble death of a beloved son must embitter the evening of her life and bring down her gray hair with sorrow to the grave…I was permitted…to write to my poor mother…I informed her of my distressed and perilous situation. I besought her to use her influence on my behalf. I waited for sometime in dreadful suspense and counted the lingering days with great anxiety until my ears were…greeted with the cheering intelligence "Your mother has come."*

General James Wilkinson, post commandant, granted Lewis some private time with his mother. The reunion was awkward as parent and child embraced, but neither said a word for quite some time. "She reproached me not," Lewis recalled, "but the silent rebuke of her heart-searching eyes were like daggers to my soul." She had borrowed a horse to ride to the barracks and wrote letters to friends in Carlisle seeking their support in pleading his case.

Mother Lewis also delivered family records to attorneys Andrew Carothers and James Duncan proving her son was a minor when he enlisted the first

This image from a 1905 postcard shows the guardhouse at Carlisle Barracks that was built by Hessian prisoners of war in 1777.

time. Her hope was that the evidence would secure his release, but a local judge ruled the civil courts had no jurisdiction in the case. Many appeals by influential residents convinced Wilkinson to commute the death sentence to prolonged confinement in the barracks' guardhouse. It would not last. Lewis had other plans.

A week into his sentence, all his restraints were removed except for a heavy chain, which was fastened to his ankle and weighed down by a thirty- to forty-pound cannonball. Lewis used a knife smuggled into his cell to saw through enough of the chain to break it off and make good his escape at the first opportunity. For fun and to stay fit, Lewis would do somersaults, always careful to keep the partially severed chain hidden from the sentry who delighted in his feats of agility.

It is said that Lewis the Robber had natural charm and leadership ability. The April 14, 1816 edition of the *Bedford Gazette* described him as a six-foot-tall, slim individual with a ruddy complexion, large sandy whiskers and blonde hair. This runs contrary to how Lewis was described in later years when he was regarded as polite in manners but serious in conversation. Lewis, however, was so successful in gaining the trust of the guard that the soldier decided not to accompany him on leave outside the stockade.

Lewis escaped and headed toward a cave just north of Carlisle, but his path was blocked by a stream. Running at full speed, the fugitive tried to clear it in one leap, but his foot slipped, and he fell against a rock on the opposite bank and received a minor sprain. He just made it to the cave mouth as the sun was setting on the waters of the nearby Conodoguinet Creek. What happened next appears in his confession: "I lost no time in entering and without the aid of candle or torch made my way as well as I could to the furthest corner of this dark and dismal place…I crept on my hands and knees through a small crevice, until I found myself in a place called the Devil's Dining Room."

He remained hidden until about 10:00 p.m., when hunger pains forced him out of the cave in search of food. Under the cover of darkness, Lewis made his way north until he came to the home of a local woman who felt sorry for him and offered Lewis a late supper of sausage, bread and cheese. Fear of being noticed prompted him to leave at about 4:00 a.m. without telling her goodbye. The cave that once had a reputation as a rendezvous for thieves is now part of the fifteen-acre Cave Hill Nature Center established by Carlisle Borough in 1963.

On his way north, Lewis met a tin peddler from Vermont, and the two became traveling companions. The peddler confided in Lewis that he was an agent for a band of counterfeiters who operated throughout the Northeast and Canada. The man invited the fugitive to join the gang, and soon Lewis was skilled in the art of making and passing bogus money. Lewis was arrested and put in jail in Troy, New York, after he used counterfeit bills to purchase a horse from an army general.

Lewis soon noticed that a young woman living across the street from his barred window kept looking at him. It turned out that Melinda had fallen in love with the rogue, and Lewis, of course, turned on the charm by convincing her that he was innocent, a victim of injustice. Melinda believed his story and talked her friend (the jailer's daughter) into leaving the cell door open after delivering the Sunday evening meal. Lewis escaped with Melinda into the night, and they were later married in Albany.

When criminal enterprise led Lewis to Manhattan, the wily con man hobnobbed with the rich and powerful. One day in 1815, Lewis managed to gain entry into an auction house disguised as a gentleman dandy. His target was Sarah Todd Astor, wife of John Jacob, one of the wealthiest men in town. Blending into the crowd, Lewis noticed how the socialite recklessly abandoned her velvet bag of jewelry and lace on a chair to talk with her admirers. In one version of this story, Lewis lifted the bag and left while Sarah was distracted. In a different version, Lewis managed to convince the rich but gullible auction patrons to trust him with their possessions in light of a recent crime spree. Both stories end with Lewis being severely beaten by fellow gang members after he removed some lace from the bag to give to his wife and did not disclose the theft to them. His gesture of love violated rules that were allegedly written down using the blood of the hardened criminals as ink.

While in Philadelphia, Lewis conspired with other criminals to kidnap local millionaire Stephen Girard and hold him for ransom. There was also talk of breaking into Girard's bank through the sewer or by digging a tunnel from Dock Street. Before any plan could be completed, Lewis was called to New Brunswick, New Jersey, after receiving word his wife and child were very ill.

Later in life, Lewis returned to his native Cumberland County, where he had several hideouts from which to base a criminal enterprise. One such refuge was a single-story log home along Hanover Street in Carlisle near the corner of South Street. At times, the presence of authorities forced Lewis and his men to vacate the home and retreat to Cave Hill where, it is said, the band of outlaws stashed away some of their loot in its many passageways. Another hideout was a hut on South Mountain where Lewis and his men printed out batches of counterfeit $100 bills. An outcropping above the Tumbling Run is still called "Lewis Rocks."

From 1816 to 1820, Lewis hid from justice in a cave overlooking a hotel in the Doubling Gap north of Newville. A favorite stop for travelers on the road to Bloomfield, the hotel was operated by Nicholas Howard, a close friend of Lewis's. As the story goes, the clever thief maintained good relations with his immediate neighbors by vowing never to rob them. In exchange, they sheltered the robber and even supplied Lewis with food and other necessities. They may have been swayed by his natural charm and by his alleged credo to only steal from corrupt officials and the very wealthy. Lewis summarized his motives in his confession:

> If there was any class of people from whom I would sooner have robbed, it was those who held public office and under color of law have been guilty of extortion…have plundered the poor and cheated the widow and the orphan. Against such workers of inequity, my mind had taken a set and I was determined never to spare them on any occasion.
>
> The groans of the distressed rang in my ears and called aloud for vengeance. There was perhaps no part of the state where I heard more complaints of this sort than in the county of Cumberland. Instead of committing a wrong, I conceive that I would be rendering society a service by punishing those official marauders who infest the town…and make the cruel feel the pains they gave.

Howard participated in this neighborhood conspiracy by hanging a red flag in a hotel window to signal Lewis whenever authorities were nosing around. When the coast was clear, he would hang a white flag, and Lewis often left his cave to visit the hotel. There, the noble bandit would party into the night with his neighbors, including Robert Moffitt. Local historian Conway Wing described Moffitt as "an old, crooked-eyed queer-looking man who frightened children with his antics." Despite appearances, Moffitt was kindhearted and actually lived in the cave with Lewis periodically over a span of six to eight months. He had this to say about the legendary criminal and other residents of Doubling Gap:

> *Lewis was a great favorite with the ladies. Some of them used to furnish us with the comforts of life, and several times visited us at the cave. We had a number of little parties at the tavern and great times...We would have every now and then a dance. This was the way we carried on whenever Lewis was here. We lived on what we got...and whatever was brought to us. I shall never forget the kindness of the people.*

This circa 1910 photograph by Maynard Hoover shows the cave in Doubling Gap that Lewis the Robber used as a hideout.

When it comes to Lewis the Robber, it can be hard to sort fact from folklore, especially when interpreting stories about his alleged kindness toward the downtrodden and God-fearing. In one such case, Lewis was preparing to rob a Newville-area family but stopped himself after hearing their voices downstairs praying for him, the intruder upstairs. Another story involved an encounter Lewis had with a man driving racehorses to the Carlisle Fair. "Do ya mind if I ride along?" Lewis asked the man. "No," the man said. As they traveled through the countryside, Lewis turned to his companion and asked, "Ain't you afraid to ride with me?" "No," the man said, "I know who I am riding with." The two struck up a conversation, during which the man told Lewis that he was poor and that his horses were not good enough to win races. "I hit a lucky streak once in a while, but please don't hold me up when I leave the fair," the man begged. "I got a wife and a family and I got to make a living." Lewis allegedly responded, "OK, I'll keep you in mind," and did not rob the luckless man.

Not all the stories of Lewis end on a positive note. In his confession, the criminal explained how he narrowly avoided jail time in Carlisle after first indulging in "the flowing bowl and sparkling glass" of excessive alcohol consumption. "Drunkenness was by no means my destroying sin or prevailing vice," Lewis said. Instead, he only got wasted "when I happen to mix with jovial company" or when he needed to drown "the clamors of remorse and the stings of conscience." One morning while traveling, Lewis visited a tavern and had a few too many.

His plan that day was to visit a shopkeeper named Martin in the village of Walnut Bottom so he could purchase goods using counterfeit money. Instead of simply paying for the goods, Lewis "acted with such impudence in the negotiation" that he aroused the suspicion of Martin, who accused Lewis of passing funny money. In the heat of their argument, Lewis proposed accompanying Martin to Carlisle to submit the bills to the inspection of bank officers. When the bills were laid before the cashier and clerk, they both agreed the money was bogus. Further investigation by town officials convinced Lewis it was time for him to leave Carlisle.

Seeing that these men "appeared to be green hands at catching a rogue," Lewis insisted he was innocent and claimed an acquaintance in town could vouch for his honesty. The men foolishly trusted Lewis and let him search for his friend unescorted. Seizing the opportunity, Lewis fled down Hanover Street, went around a street corner and eventually hid out in a cave until early the next morning, when he snuck out of town.

Lewis was not so lucky in April 1820, when he was part of a plot to rob a wealthy farmer in East Pennsboro Township. Planning for that crime began after Lewis and fellow gang members were in a local tavern and overheard neighborhood residents describe the farmer as having more money than all the rest of the farmers put together. Unfortunately for Lewis, the neighbors also noticed a group of strangers in the neighborhood several times in the weeks leading up to the robbery. Suspicious, they instructed the wife of the wealthy farmer to blow a horn to summon help if intruders came onto her property.

Sure enough, an attempt was made but foiled after the woman sounded the alarm. Reflecting later on the incident, Lewis said the farmer's wife displayed as much courage as any man in the face of danger. Lewis was arrested and remanded to the county jail in Carlisle, only to be transferred to the Franklin County Jail in Chambersburg, reputed to be the most fortified in Pennsylvania at that time. He managed to escape through trickery and to continue his life of crime for almost three months before fate finally caught up with the legend.

As the story goes, Lewis and an accomplice named Connolly robbed a small wagon train in the Seven Mountains in what is now Centre County, Pennsylvania. A posse tracked the two men up the Driftwood branch of the Sinnemahoning Creek, where the criminals were surrounded. When the posse demanded their surrender, the desperadoes shouted back, "Shoot and be damned!" Lewis took a bullet in the arm while Connolly was mortally wounded in the abdomen and would die later that day. Lewis was taken captive and imprisoned in the county jail at Bellefonte where he died on July 13, 1820, and was buried in the Baptist cemetery at Milesburg. Some believe there may yet be buried treasure hidden by Lewis somewhere in the caves outside Carlisle, the hills outside Bellefonte and in Vermont's Smugglers Notch.

There is evidence to suggest the confession was a political ploy hatched by James Duncan, the Cumberland County attorney who was influential in saving Lewis from the death penalty while he was imprisoned at Carlisle Barracks. Duncan was a supporter of Joseph Hiester in his 1820 race for Pennsylvania governor against a hugely popular William Findlay, the incumbent who had at one point pardoned Lewis from serving out a ten-year prison sentence.

Duncan went to Bellefonte to see Lewis, who was dying of his wounds. There, Duncan convinced the career criminal to make a confession with the understanding that it would be published. Duncan then edited the material and distributed the confession to areas hard hit by the exploits of Lewis and his gang. The idea was to show that Findlay was responsible for years of criminal activity that could have been prevented, had the request for a pardon been denied. The ploy worked. Findlay was defeated, and Duncan was made auditor general under the Hiester administration. In the following excerpt, Lewis described his motive behind the confession:

> *I have already sinned so much against heaven and earth, against God and my country, the only reparation I can make is to give a full disclosure… of my manifold crimes…nor do I think the atonement would be complete unless I strip the veil from my heart and expose every secret intention and declare with truth and candor all the plans and schemes…*
>
> *I trust I will have the effect to deter youth and others from adopting… the same course of life in which I embarked and, by exhibiting myself as a beacon, I can warn others from the dangerous shoals in which I have shipwrecked my own happiness and peace of mind.*

Part II

Cruel Days

No doubt, Dickinson College has endured as a positive draw and influence that has helped to shape the community for well over two hundred years; yet there exists a history of tension brewing just beneath the surface, as evidenced by two violent episodes from the nineteenth century that pitted students against townsfolk. Then again, mischief is common in any college town. Why should Carlisle be any different? Young minds need a relief valve from serious studies. Vexing problems beget creative solutions in the form of clever pranks that laid low an unpopular college president and made an alluring figure of mythology an object of unwanted attention. Part II closes with the story of a federal investigation into how a social experiment in Native American policy was betrayed by its own hype and made dysfunctional.

A Passion to Tatters

Town-Gown Troubles

There were reports the students had armed themselves with pistols, knives and clubs. About one hundred youths had gathered on May 1, 1843, to force the town militia off the Dickinson College campus. They had succeeded only to be driven back beyond the stone wall by the point of the bayonet. There, the students held their ground against the reinforced infantry company until the arrival of artillery from Carlisle Barracks convinced them to retreat back to their rooms. They had left behind a bloody Waterloo of wounded on both sides, but it was said the carnage could have been far worse had the militia been issued ammunition.

There's more to the crisis: Infantry officers together with army privates were reportedly taken prisoner during the melee. That night, at about ten o'clock, a rescue attempt was thwarted by a strong guard the sheriff had on duty at the jail. The *Spirit of the Times*, a Philadelphia newspaper, mentioned how patrols walked the streets amid a climate of great excitement. It was curious how such a gross exaggeration could be accepted as truth by journalists, far removed from what actually happened.

There was a confrontation that day between students and the militia, but the only casualties were hurt feelings and wounded pride. The one instance of physical violence involved a soldier who fired a musket in the direction of his tormenters. Reports in Carlisle newspapers say nothing of a pitched battle on campus except for what was published in Philadelphia and Baltimore. The incident sparked an exchange of scathing criticism between George Sanderson, editor of the *American Volunteer*, and his counterpart, Captain E. Beatty of the *Carlisle Herald & Expositor*.

For weeks, the two editors colored the facts in opinion columns about the college affair. From the start, Sanderson had a personal bias as the commander of the militia company involved in the confrontation. His opening salvo entitled "Blackguardism" hints of underlying class warfare and of the animosity that existed between townsfolk and college students. Sanderson described the soldiers as "working men" who "from necessity of choice" were "engaged in laudable employment earning a livelihood by the sweat of their brows." He goes on to add, "They will never permit the ill-bred haughty scions of purse-proud and bloated aristocracy to wantonly… insult them with impunity. We hope never to see again an attempt made to sport with the feelings of our citizens' soldiery."

Sanderson explained how soldiers marching south along North West Street from Louther Street to High Street were "grossly insulted" by students occupying the East College building. They yelled "taunts, jeers and other ruffian-like [remarks]" at the infantry, prompting a soldier to load his musket with a ball cartridge and open fire. The shot missed, but to Sanderson, it had the effect of showing the students how their disgraceful behavior would not be tolerated. In defending the college, Sanderson explained how the student misconduct took place when none of the professors were on campus. He mentioned how one faculty member even expressed regret over what had happened.

The *Herald* took issue with how Sanderson justified the hostile gunfire as necessary to prove a point. "However reprehensible [was] the conduct of the students, the conduct of the soldiers was infinitely worse," Beatty wrote. "What is the individual to be coolly shot down in the street who dares to laugh at whatever may happen to excite his visible organs? What a monstrous assumption in this free country." Beatty went on to say that Sanderson "tore a passion to tatters" in the abuse he vented on students, on whom he "cast an unmerited stigma" and did "great injury to an institution which our citizens cherish."

While the *Herald* agreed that the soldiers were insulted, the paper argued it would have been more appropriate for the men to suffer in silence and then report "the mere boys" to college authorities. The rival newspaper stated only five to six of the younger students actually committed the deed. The *Herald* also took aim at Sanderson himself with the following: "Our neighbor's military enthusiasm certainly got the better of his democracy. His head has been filled with visions of the glorious practice of monarchial governments where standing armies are kept up to compel the people into submission."

Dickinson College students relax outside their dormitory rooms at the East College building, circa 1890.

On May 18, 1843, the *Volunteer* published a revised version of what happened the day of the incident. Sanderson claimed at least fifty students were involved and all were men old enough to know how to behave. Instead, the students used foul language in hurling insults at passing soldiers from the upper-story windows. "In this free country, we don't recognize the right of any class to ride roughshod over their more humble fellows," Sanderson wrote. "We have no desire to injure the character of the college in anything we have said or may have yet to say on the subject. Our only motive is to hold up the reprehensible conduct of these young men, not mere boys, so they be ashamed of it themselves and conduct themselves more like gentlemen."

Sanderson believed that while the *Herald* was making excuses for the students, most residents condemned the conduct of these "upstarts from other states" because it insulted not only the soldiers but also civilians living in Carlisle. He claimed dozens witnessed the behavior. "We hope we are now done with this unpleasant subject," Sanderson wrote. But that was not to be the case.

On May 24, the *Herald* reprinted the battle version of the college affair as published in the big city newspapers. Beatty called it both a hoax dreamed up in the imagination and the "frightful intelligence of a desperate Waterloo engagement." For once, the rival editors could agree. "The editor of the *Spirit of the Times* has been made the silly dupe of a vile hoax under the cover of a heap of foul abuse upon our humble self, the officers and members of the infantry and the working class of the borough," Sanderson wrote in a May 25 editorial.

Sanderson added that any abuse heaped upon him was of no consequence, "nor do I care a straw for it. We are accustomed to be bespattered with such fish-woman slang." For him, it was an honor to command the Carlisle Infantry—the oldest organized corps of volunteers in the state and the second oldest in the country, according to Sanderson. "For sixty years, it has been the pride and the boast of the town," he wrote. "Many of the oldest and most respectable of our citizens were once members of the company." He mentioned how the unit served with George Washington during the Whiskey Rebellion and campaigned for six months in the northern frontier and Canada during the War of 1812. "The company always enjoyed the confidence of this community."

This muster notice for the Carlisle Infantry, dated April 28, 1824, is part of the library collection at the Cumberland County Historical Society.

CARLISLE INFANTRY.

YOU are ordered to parade, at the court house in the borough of Carlisle, on MONDAY,

The 3d of May next,

precisely at *nine o'clock*, A. M in Summer Uniform, arms and accoutrements in good order.

ALSO

On Monday the 10th of May, at the same hour, both being days appointed by law.

EDWARD ARMOR, Capt.

April 28, 1824.

Sanderson believed the battle version may have been concocted by the "aristocratic fledglings" of Dickinson College. He called the behavior "pointless ridicule of blackguard abuse" by a "set of brainless insolent upstarts who are a disgrace to any institution of learning and is there to sink the character of this Dickinson College below the standard of contempt." As for the *Herald*, Beatty wrote that his reprinting of the battle version was not done to prolong the controversy with the *Volunteer*. "Our neighbor is very sensitive on the subject and the magnitude of the indignity increases the more he thinks about it." However, the *Herald* was not about to change its opinion that Sanderson overreacted. "We still believe he would have acted a more dignified part in passing the matter over in silence."

Forty-five years later, another confrontation erupted between Dickinson College students and local volunteers serving to protect Carlisle. As before, there were conflicting versions of what went on, along with a lively debate in local newspapers over who displayed the worst behavior. Once again, there are inklings of underlying class warfare between students and townsfolk and implications that college youth were being disrespectful of the toils of the average working man. Both incidents took place in the exact same location on campus—only what happened on Halloween night in 1888 was no hoax or exaggeration. The students actually fought a pitched battle, during which people were injured on both sides, not by bullets or bayonets, but by sticks and stones.

It began while most borough residents were in bed asleep. They were startled from slumber by the sudden cry of "Fire!" A *Carlisle Herald* reporter described the scene:

> *The clash of bells, the loud rumble and clatter of the hose trucks and engines as they were rushed over the stony streets combined with the cries and shouts of the men and boys hurrying along was sure to awoke the soundest sleeper…and, in a twinkling, every household was astir and the anxious inquiry "Where is it?" was heard from the windows of dwellings along the street.*

Town residents had their answer in the form of a bright light illuminating West High Street. The fear at first was that a building was ablaze, but people soon realized it was a bonfire set by college students. Trouble began after firefighters connected a hose to a hydrant at North West Street before entering the campus. They were immediately set upon by students who viewed the first responders as intruders and tried to remove them from the grounds. What followed was a forty-five-minute brawl where both students and firefighters exchanged body blows and pitched stones at each other, causing several injuries.

One stone struck a Union Fire Company officer on the left temple, causing a large gash on his head that required medical attention. The *Herald* reported how a second firefighter was hit in the arm, while a third received a blow to the stomach. As for the students, one was struck in the face by a stone, which knocked out several teeth, while another was severely manhandled during the struggle for control of the hose nozzle. The students took over at one point and directed the nozzle and its water at the firemen before they tossed the length of hose over the stone wall. It was later recovered by the firefighters who pressed on, reinforced by other men arriving on the scene.

The firemen pushed their way farther onto the campus by using the hose to drench a number of students. Though some students resorted to wearing rubber coats, it was not enough to protect them from the spray, so they retreated to a safe distance where they heaped verbal abuse upon the heads of the firefighters. The *Herald* reporter wrote that as stones continued to whiz through campus, the midnight air was "made hideous with the shouts of the contending parties." Ironically, not a single drop of water was actually directed onto the fire until it had almost burned itself out.

In a November 1, 1888 article, the *Herald* published its impressions of the public's reaction of what had happened the night before. While a few of the residents objected to the firemen rigging a hose and entering the campus, the opinion of the majority was that their actions were right and proper, according to the newspaper. "No town in Pennsylvania had a better fire department than Carlisle," the article read. "All companies are composed of reputable citizens always ready and eager to respond to the call when a building is in danger."

Both the *Herald* and the *Evening Sentinel* cited student behavior as the root cause of the tension leading up to the Halloween incident. They reported how, for many years, the students had raised false fire alarms or set nuisance fires throughout the campus, usually late at night or in the early-morning hours. This happened so often that it disrupted the sleep patterns of volunteer firefighters, annoyed to the point where they threatened vengeance and vowed to put an end to the mischief.

The *Herald* was concerned false alarms by students could put the neighborhoods adjoining the campus in jeopardy. Firemen believing the alarm was just a prank may hesitate to run a call on West High Street or wait too long to verify that the fire was genuine. "No one could condemn them when it is taken into consideration how often they have been by their eagerness made dupes" by the maliciousness of students, the *Herald* said.

The *Sentinel* also sided with the firefighters, saying they had every right to enter the campus and put out a fire that violated a ban on bonfires within borough limits. Students got the worst of it when their interference only made the firefighters more determined. "If students stopped the false alarm business, the firemen would never molest them." The *Sentinel* suggested the students advise authorities ahead of time whenever they plan to set a bonfire during the course of celebrating.

On November 2, the *Sentinel* published an editorial written by a Dickinson College senior. In it, the student claimed the *Herald* distorted the facts and made the "prime movers" appear as heroes while the students were branded as malicious disturbers of the peace. "There are two sides to every question," the student said. "Let us examine the facts and judge whether the firemen or the students were the real offenders."

The senior explained how acting college president Charles Francis Himes had talked to students after the morning chapel service. Himes announced plans to put up a new fence along the part of the campus facing College Street. He asked students to find a way to eliminate the remnants of the old fence. The students decided to burn it in celebration of Halloween. They started tearing it down at about 10:30 p.m., stacking the wood in a pile at the center of the campus. The match was lit and cheers echoed through the streets as students danced around the bonfire. The celebration lasted about ten minutes before an alarm bell was heard coming from the Union Fire Station about three blocks away. Firefighters quickly arrived on the scene.

The senior described how volunteers quickly connected the hose to the hydrant at the corner of North West and West High Streets. A crowd of men and boys then advanced onto the campus in an act that was purely unnecessary because the fire was already going down, the senior wrote. In his opinion, the bonfire was not any more dangerous than all the rockets that were fired during the night's parade. The student speculated the reason why the firefighters entered the campus was to provoke a confrontation and follow through on the threats.

The senior wrote that it was the firefighters who cast the first stone. After the hose was turned on them, they avenged themselves by removing rocks from the nearby railroad grade. They were then reinforced by other firefighters, "numerous recruits from the roughest elements in town" and a train full of men who had just returned from Mechanicsburg. The student

Dr. Charles F. Himes, circa 1900.

claimed this mob was led by "reputable citizens," including a borough official who, instead of working to quell the disturbance, urged the rioters on. "Before those overwhelming odds, the college boys slowly withdrew. Deluged with water, with stones singing about their ears, they finally entered the college building," the senior wrote.

But the drama continued. According to the student, the firemen, together with their accomplices, stoned the college buildings until two professors convinced them to leave. The fact that the firemen had waited until after to hose down the fire proved their real motive was to incite violence and that they had regarded the fire as non-threatening. The next morning, dozens of rocks were found strewn about the ground in front of East College.

The college senior went on to claim the ban on bonfires had not been enforced for years, rendering it a dead-letter law. The police chief knew that when he came up to the students as they were dismantling the fence, the senior wrote. Rather than discourage the students, the chief said, "Go ahead; it's alright boys as long as you create no disturbance on College Street." The chief denied this version of events, saying he had no authority to grant anyone permission to violate a borough ordinance. "It is simply a question of diamond cut diamond," the *Herald* reported. "Even if the chief granted them permission, it did not make it any better for the students who remain guilty of violating the law."

Meanwhile, Chief Burgess Theodore Cornman disputed the nonenforcement claim in a letter published November 3, 1888, in the *Sentinel.* "I have enforced every ordinance and punished every violator in every instance when brought to my knowledge," Cornman wrote. He invited borough residents and college students to come forward with any information they may have regarding the Halloween incident. The assistant burgess issued a statement in response to the claim by the senior that the police chief sat atop the corner fire hydrant to block firefighters before he was jostled away by a fireman. The statement read that the chief "wished to prevent a fight he knew would occur if firemen would go upon campus to attempt to extinguish the fire."

Impulse of the Moment

Nasty College Pranks

T he fear was that the patch of loose soil concealed evidence of a terrible crime perpetrated on the Dickinson College campus. A German laborer, known only as Fred, discovered the burial plot and immediately notified authorities. Its size suggested an infant had met with foul play, prompting the coroner to impanel an inquest jury to verify whether it was homicide. Students were undoubtedly among those morbidly curious who had gathered to watch as the remains were exhumed from the shallow grave. Professor James Marshall thought it strange how so many of the young men had gleams in their eyes. His suspicions were soon confirmed when, instead of a body, workers dug up a book so drab and dusty in its contents that it bored many a student to death.

The book prank began on December 14, 1856, when Ali Slape, a college junior, snuck into a professor's room to steal a book on intellectual philosophy by Asa Mahan. At eleven o'clock the next evening, leaders in the conspiracy met in Slape's room where they placed the book, shrouded in a black cloth, upon a white window shutter that served as the bier. From there, they marched to the room of a different professor where most of the junior and senior classes had gathered to witness W.J. Stevenson deliver an elegy on Mahan, an educator, a reformer and the first president of Oberlin College.

Among the juniors was Horatio Collins King, who often instigated mischief, which he later wrote about in a journal he kept for all four of his college years. This document provides a unique insight into what it was like to be an undergraduate student in mid-nineteenth-century America. The class of 1858 enjoyed pulling pranks on faculty members in protest of boring lectures, dry sermons and the tedious practice of forcing students to recite passages from textbooks. In his journal, King wrote how he came to the ceremony dressed in "my long patriarchal cloak and a black sailor's hat fixed in imitation of a priest's three-cornered affair." With a long black cape and hood hiding all but his face, King thought he looked the part of a clergyman officiating over a funeral service.

After the elegy, a different student read a poem (which King described as "very appropriate with a number of good bits") before the procession re-formed with six pallbearers taking the lead. King was next followed by fellow juniors and the senior class—half of which had members holding lamps and candles. The students marched down West High Street to the campus gate where they entered and walked to the southwest corner of the campus where the hole had been dug. King described what happened next:

> *First an ode to the tune of Auld Lang Syne was sung with spirit. I read my sermon of fifteen minutes length during which the coffin was lowered and the earth dropped lightly in. Cloud delivered an appropriate Latin prayer which was very good indeed. We then sang the second ode to the tune of Massa's in the Cold, Cold Ground. I sang the solo and all joined in the chorus. I then pronounced the blessing and we all started towards our rooms yelling and howling most piteously.*

This was, of course, a complete sham. The students were faking sorrow over what King had called "an abominable bore." "To think of it as defunct sends a thrill of pleasure to the heart," he wrote. "Farewell old Mahan: May you lie forever in that chilly grave undisturbed, unchanged." But alas, it was not meant to be forever. Fearing the worst, Carlisle residents had unwittingly disinterred the bane of Dickinson College students.

The journal mentioned other pranks in which King was involved. In one case, students stole tallow from the pantry of his uncle and college president Charles Collins. They then smeared the tallow on a blackboard to render it useless for twelve hours. Another popular target were the classroom stoves, which pranksters either dismantled, poured water into or spiked with red pepper to make the air intolerable to breathe.

Sometime during his junior or senior year, King stopped pulling pranks and instead became annoyed by the deeds of the underclassmen. Apparently, he began to see the difference between harmless practical jokes that rattled nerves and vandalism that crippled day-to-day college operations. In the second semester of his junior year, King wrote how this willful damaging of property was "devoid of keenness and shows a bad spirit in the perpetrators." An 1858 graduate, he would serve in the Civil War and became a lawyer, a leader and an organizer. An avid music lover, King was once the director of the Philharmonic Society of Brooklyn and chairman of its music committee. He also composed music, including the college alma mater, "Noble Dickinsonia."

As for his uncle, Dr. Collins was not bothered by pranksters and knew just how to push back to make a point. When students tried to drown out his chapel speeches by foot stomping, Collins just stood there and refused to speak until the students decided to calm down. Sometimes, he would force them to sit for hours at evening services until they learned their lesson. While his predecessor, Jessie Truesdell Peck, was indecisive and erratic in his handling of discipline, Collins was firm but rational, enabling him to develop a positive relationship with the student body.

When Robert Emory died in Baltimore on May 18, 1848, Peck was chosen to replace him as Dickinson College president. The college at the time was affiliated with the Methodist faith. Peck had a fine record as both a minister and the head of two seminaries, but from the beginning, students viewed him in contrast to Emory, who was beloved and admired by the campus community. Although educated, Peck was not a college man, so he lacked insight going into the office on September 18, 1848.

Jessie Truesdell Peck. *Courtesy of Dickinson College Library and Information Services.*

His appearance and personality made Peck an easy target for some of the nastiest student pranks ever perpetrated in Dickinson College history. He was described as a massive figure who strutted around campus with his huge belly protruding like a peacock's tail on display. Dignified in bearing, Peck had a strange habit of rolling his r's in conversation, but what got him into trouble the most was his attitude toward the students. One of those who took aim at Peck was Moncure Conway, class of 1849, who, years after his legendary prank, wrote, "Our immature minds could not appreciate his good qualities, while his large paunch, fat face, baby-like baldness and pompous air impressed the whole college as a caricature. He had been a school teacher, and called us boys, and we felt he was inclined to discipline us like boys."

Conway would confess to being the only culprit in a scheme that had Peck committed to an insane asylum on March 7, 1849. Conway claimed he was seeking revenge for his friend, Henry Smith, being brought before the faculty and punished for drinking and playing cards. "Smith had become intoxicated under the impulse of the moment," Conway wrote. Though Smith was later returned to class after a plea from his mother and a pledge of good behavior, Conway wrote that the whole incident "stirred my dislike of Peck into wrath."

As the story goes, Conway hatched a plot one evening while playing euchre with two friends. Their conversation turned to Peck's upcoming trip to Staunton, Virginia, to give a report on Dickinson College before an annual regional conference of Methodist leaders. Peck had also made arrangements to witness the inauguration of President Zachary Taylor in Washington, D.C.

Conway saw his chance for payback. He knew Staunton was famous for its asylum, which had a physician named Stribling as its superintendent. Using an assumed name, Conway wrote Stribling a letter explaining how a harmless lunatic who imagined himself Dickinson College's president had run away to Staunton to make a report to the conference. In his letter, Conway described Peck in great detail and asked Stribling to please detain the poor soul until friends could come for him. "I could not suppose that this…would have any result beyond raising a laugh on him; but Peck was met by Stribling in his carriage," Conway wrote.

Peck arrived in Staunton as scheduled. After stepping off the train, he was approached by a man seeking to confirm his identity. Peck confirmed he was the president of Dickinson College, and the stranger invited Peck to step inside the carriage. Believing it to be a courtesy extended to guests at the conference, Peck complied and was driven to the asylum while he continued to chat with his travel companion. Only later did he realize where he had been taken and demanded he be released. Stribling kept reassuring Peck he would not be harmed. The protests got so loud that Stribling sent for people at the conference to come and identify Peck. When the asylum finally released Peck, Stribling apologized for the misunderstanding.

Peck's trip was ruined, and a subsequent investigation failed to identify Conway as the culprit. Nine months later, in December 1849, students again played a nasty trick on Peck. This time, the college president was locked inside a freight car overnight. At that time, the Cumberland Valley Railroad had a track running down the middle of West High Street and a siding along the front of the campus. Boxcars parked there were often broken into by students who stole food.

One night, Peck could hear students whispering just outside his office about a plot to pilfer some oysters from one of the boxcars. The students hurried off, opened the side door and ducked under the car to await the

This 1879 photograph by Charles Himes shows the Cumberland Valley Railroad siding in front of the Dickinson College campus. Old West, the main administrative building, sits in the background.

arrival of Peck. When the president appeared and called out to them, they made noises as though they were inside the boxcar. Peck climbed inside only to have the door closed and locked behind him. At that point, the students pushed the car over the grade at West Street, and the car coasted by gravity down to the bridge over the Letort Creek. Peck was confined for hours before anyone investigated the contents of the boxcar.

The following January, someone shot Peck's dog, causing Peck to demand that all students surrender their firearms at the next chapel service. The students showed up but instead dumped tongs, pokers and shovels from every stove on campus at Peck's feet. Not only was Peck unpopular with students, but he also lacked fundraising ability at a time when the college really needed the money. Though he visited churches and camp meetings, he always came up short. Enrollment declined by nearly a third during his administration from 158 students in the 1847–48 academic year to 107 when he left in July 1852. In June 1851, Peck tendered his resignation effective at the close of the 1851–52 year with the following comments: "I have been for sometime convinced my happiness and usefulness and perhaps my health and life would require me to change my field and kind of labor in as early a period of time as possible. I have determined to follow strictly the indication of providence and seek rest from cares and labors to which I feel myself poorly adapted."

Despite this announcement, the pranks continued up until the end. In May 1852, students set fire to the outhouse adjoining the president's home. This was done as Peck was writing his final commencement address. Peck would have greater success later in life as a bishop of the Methodist Episcopal Church and as one of the founders in 1870 of Syracuse University. But there was at least one other story that connected Peck to Dickinson College. Sometime in the 1860s, Peck was strolling on the deck of a Mississippi steamboat when he heard a familiar ring. He investigated and found out the signal was coming from the same bell that had gone missing from Old West, the main administrative building on campus. It is said that Peck had the captain return the bell, which the college must have fastened more securely because only the clapper kept disappearing in the years that followed.

Atop the cupola that housed the bell was a weather vane in the shape of a mermaid. Historians disagree on her origins. Dr. Charles Sellers wrote how Benjamin Latrobe, architect of Old West, wanted to add the figure of Triton, the fish-tailed god of wind and sea, as the weather vane, but the Carlisle coppersmith who hammered it into shape was more familiar with mermaids than Greek gods. Professor Charles Himes wrote how the weather vane was really the idea of Dr. Charles Nisbet, the first president of

This 1895 photograph by Charles Himes shows the mermaid weather vane atop the cupola on Old West at Dickinson College.

Dickinson College, who probably didn't have a mermaid in mind.

Regardless of where she came from, her destiny was to seduce generations of college students eager to prove their ingenuity in finding ways to kidnap her. Who can say what was most attractive—the black curls, the golden body, the green tail—but her mere presence inspired men to leap from a tree on the south side of the building. Her admirers, however, were far from gentle in their nefarious pursuits. A new dent appeared on her body almost every time she was abducted. She was usually kept hidden until enough outrage had risen, and then she would reappear in an office or back on her perch.

For years, it was a school tradition for the mermaid to be stolen early in the semester and then returned during the homecoming football game. This trend continued until the fall of 1967 when she disappeared for months, only to turn up the following spring in a New York City apartment. It is said her kidnapper was threatened with criminal charges if he did not arrange for her return. President Howard Lane Rubendall then decided it was time for the mermaid to be placed in a more secure location. A flat silhouette now sits atop the cupola, replacing the original weather vane, which is now displayed in the Waidner-Spahr Library.

There is at least one story of the mermaid being an accomplice to a crime committed much earlier in her history. One day, students stole the bicycle of a local chaplain and managed to sneak it intact into the bottom of the cupola. When they found that the bike was too large to maneuver through the opening, the students dismantled it and then reassembled it on the roof, hanging the bike from the mermaid's tail. The stunt cost the college money because it had to hire a steeplejack from Harrisburg to lower the bicycle to the ground.

False Fabric...Liquor Evil

Indian School Woes

The thrashing began with a slap across the face that brought Julia Hardin to her knees. To ward off further blows, the orphan threw up her hands to cover her head, but Claude Stauffer pushed her over and started to spank the eighteen-year-old woman. Partway through the punishment, the band director switched to a makeshift paddle—the dimensions of which were unclear given conflicting testimony before the congressional committee investigating allegations of wrongdoing at the Carlisle Indian Industrial School. The politicians were horrified by the statements they heard about the level of violence and the evidence of an attempted cover-up.

Witnesses agreed that, in June 1913, Hardin was steadfast in her refusal to sign a check to debit her savings toward the payment of transportation costs to her Outing home. For years, the school had offered a program where qualified students were sent out into the countryside to work for families, earn money and learn a trade. Hardin told school officials she lacked the proper clothing and did not have a suitcase or trunk to carry her things. Her refusal to budge prompted Matron Hannah Ridenour to report the matter to school Superintendent Moses Friedman.

Friedman directed Stauffer to try to convince Hardin to sign the paperwork. He failed and, upon returning to Friedman, suggested that the young woman get a spanking. "What she needs is a good straightening out," Stauffer reportedly said. "Why don't you give it to her?" Friedman replied. Hardin was escorted into a room where the blinds were drawn, and she was again confronted with the demand to comply with the Outing request. Hardin refused, held her ground and paid for it.

Before committee members, she testified that Stauffer struck her forty to fifty times about the head, shoulders and back with a paddle about four inches wide and two and a half feet long. Hardin also claimed that Stauffer threw her to the floor multiple times during the thrashing and that she was being held down by the matron. In his version of what happen, Stauffer said he hit the girl lightly only ten to twelve times using a piece of wood one foot long, two inches wide and a quarter inch thick. The incident ended when Principal John Whitwell arrived on the scene and persuaded Hardin to do as she was told.

Sometime later, Hardin was pressured by Ridenour to sign a piece of paper, the contents of which were a mystery to the student. Hardin was not given the opportunity to study the document closely, nor were any of its statements read to her. This was done inside the matron's room in the presence of a notary public. Two more times, Ridenour brought Hardin to her room and tried to get the young woman to sign additional papers, but she refused. Hardin had since learned the first piece of paper was a fake letter that expressed her remorse for her misdeed and thanked Stauffer for what he had done to set her straight.

Claude Stauffer, band director at the Carlisle Indian Industrial School.

The Hardin case was brought to the attention of E.B. Linnen, an inspector with the Federal Bureau of Indian Affairs. He had arrived on campus in January 1914 under orders to investigate reports of misconduct. Linnen obtained a written statement from Stauffer, who later refused to sign the affidavit and instead insulted the inspector. This prompted Linnen to charge

Stauffer with insubordination and to recommend that the band director be removed from that department. Linnen also suggested that Ridenour be reassigned because her harsh treatment of Indian girls had strained her relationship with the student body.

The thrashing of Julia Hardin stood out as an extreme example of how the campus suffered from so much low morale and dysfunction, which set students on the verge of a rebellion by early 1914. The school began as a social experiment to assimilate native boys and girls into the white man's culture. Founder Richard Pratt believed the best way to civilize the Indians was to take their children away from tribal influences and put them among the white man to learn a useful trade.

A veteran soldier, Pratt lobbied the Department of the Interior to get Carlisle Barracks on loan from the War Department. The army had closed the post in 1871 due to its small size and the poor relationship the garrison had with local residents. Pratt had no problem garnering local support. Merchants missed the money soldiers used to spend in town. The school that first opened in October 1879 flourished to nearly one thousand students and fielded athletic teams that competed against the nation's leading colleges. The success of Jim Thorpe as one of the country's greatest all-around athletes brought even more fame to the school. But all this renown came with a price.

This circa 1908 photograph by Everett Strong shows the main entrance to the Carlisle Indian Industrial School on Pratt Avenue. Coach Glenn Warner's home was the first to the right of the entrance.

As time went by, the student body got progressively older. By 1914, the average age was seventeen or eighteen, meaning students were well in their twenties by graduation. These older students not only brought with them adjustment issues but also greater emotional baggage, including previous exposure to sex and alcohol—two vices in abundance in the seedy neighborhoods close to the school. This was compounded by an approach to discipline that treated adults as if they were children.

Students were under constant surveillance by school officials, and any violation of the rules could result in a number of punishments depending on the severity of the offense and the student's prior record. These included barring the student from on-campus social activities, having their off-campus privileges revoked, suspension from class and confinement in the school lockup on bread and water rations. Conditions on campus drove some students to break the rules and commit crimes just to be removed from the school.

In November 1897, Lizzie Flanders and Fannie Eaglehorn were expelled after a judge sentenced them both to eighteen months in state prison for twice attempting to set fire to the girls' quarters. In February 1915, a rather homesick Newton Robinson used oil-soaked rags to try and burn down the industrial shops. He would later escape from the school lockup only to be caught again trying to ignite a different school building. Robinson was remanded to Cumberland County Jail pending his arson trial in March. He was found guilty and sent to a reform school.

While it was common for the Indian school to have difficult students or repeat offenders placed in the county jail, there was a case, in September 1913, when such imprisonment violated state law. Twenty-year-old Paul Jones and eighteen-year-old Ethel Williams spent seventy days in the county jail on charges of fornication—a misdemeanor offense that normally carries just a fine. While Jones spent that time in a prison cell filled with vermin and hardened criminals, the sheriff's wife took pity on Williams and spared her from filthy conditions by enlisting her help with household chores.

Male students looking for sex would often sneak off campus to solicit and befriend local prostitutes. There were even cases where students had intimate relationships with other local women and with members of their Outing host family. On April 21, 1914, students John Bear and Joseph Muggins were caught off campus and out of uniform. An investigation revealed that the men had spent the previous evening in the company of known prostitutes. When questioned, Bear vowed that no one could separate him from his lover, Hazel Meyers, who testified that she had been running around with Bear for some time. It was customary for him to pay her a dollar each time they had sex. In this way, Meyers had earned at least twenty dollars.

Just over a month after their court-martial, Bear and Muggins were briefly considered suspects in the homicide of Hazel Meyers. Her body was found in the cellar of a vacant home on the outskirts of Carlisle. The nineteen-year-old woman had been beaten to death, and her face and neck had been slashed with a knife or sharp instrument. Acting superintendent Oscar Lipps was anxious to keep the names of the two students out of the newspapers. He was further upset when journalists tried to link Indian students from the school to the murder. "Press correspondents should have care when writing of anything local and not rush into print...reports, rumors and theories that are not only ludicrous but bring the town into disrepute," Lipps said. Bear and Muggins were later expelled.

Alcohol consumption among students was a more serious problem. Often at night, they would sneak into town out of uniform to frequent bars or to buy liquor from bootleggers. Watchmen were ineffective because they would allow their friends to come and go as they pleased. Carlisle police didn't want to intervene because the officers felt it was not their responsibility to monitor students of a government-run school. Besides, serving alcohol to Indians was a federal offense. Town residents were torn between having to cope with intoxicated and troublesome students and the regular income the Indian school provided to the local economy.

The geography had changed from when the school first opened. Farmland around Carlisle Barracks had given way to development that, by 1910, had pushed the town limits closer to the post. The adjoining neighborhoods offered a wide variety of taverns and brothels, making it easy for enterprising students to indulge in vice. The congressional inquiry of 1914 resulted in Friedman being suspended and replaced by Lipps, who once described Carlisle as a "veritable Hell hole infested with dives and grog shops of the worst type."

Local residents were worried about the possible ramifications of the federal investigation. Advocates for sobriety equated the survival of the institution with the need for temperance. In a January 1915 editorial published in the *Sentinel*, one writer speculated how the lack of effort by the business community to wipe out saloons could spell the demise of a school that pumped thousands of dollars into the local economy every year:

> *Whenever there has been any suggestion of the removal of the Indian school...our citizens have been up in arms particularly the merchants*

who profit by its location here. There is one thing that would mitigate against keeping the school here. It is the licensed liquor traffic in Carlisle and the subsequent trail of crime and vice. The government might well hesitate to maintain schools where the surroundings are not quite what they should be.

That same month, Dr. W.A. Hutchinson, president of the county No-License League, wrote Lipps a letter asking for his opinion on whether the presence of so many drinking establishments in Carlisle presented a serious threat to the best interests of the school. Hutchinson wanted Lipps to draw on his experience as a past supervisor of similar institutions. Below are excerpts of what Lipps wrote in response:

The most serious problem confronting…my effort to reconstruct the Carlisle school along broader and more efficient lines is the local environment…with respect to moral conditions and the sale of liquor to our Indian students… [I]n no other Indian schools do we have anything like these serious problems that confront us here in Carlisle…

It will…be sufficient…to state that we are surrounded by all manner of temptation and that women of doubtful character send invitations to our boys, follow them to our very door and at every opportunity offer them inducements to violate not only the rules of the school, but the law of the land. Just how this problem can be solved, I am at a loss to even suggest…

I realize fully that the saloon is the father of vice, but the liquor evil… is not our only trouble. I regard the moral conditions…as fully destructive to the character as the liquor evil.

Conditions on campus were just as bad. Around Christmas 1914, five seventeen-year-old students broke into the school warehouse and stole a large quantity of lemon extract. They were found intoxicated in student housing. Three of the boys—Charles Wilson, Frank Young Eagle and George Roberts—armed themselves when school officials tried to force them to participate in their own court-martial. No one was hurt, and the three boys were later expelled.

School founder Richard Pratt was a teetotaler who often used his own abstinence as moral leverage to shame the student body into compliance. He would often make examples of Indians who violated the rules. Pratt also supported "a good thrashing" when corporal punishment was needed to put a disobedient student in his or her place.

As for Friedman, he drank regularly and was criticized by some for being a bad influence on the students. And yet, during the congressional hearings, local ministers and community leaders praised Friedman for his work in curbing student alcohol consumption. While Friedman publicly denounced the use of corporal punishment, testimony in the Hardin case would suggest otherwise, and there was proof senior staff members routinely violated his directive and administered such discipline without consulting him first. Friedman had other problems. A weak administrator, he became such an object of scorn that students routinely hissed at him and used anti-Semitic slurs to attack his Jewish heritage. They even threw shoes at him on one occasion.

Indian commissioner Cato Sells dispatched inspector Linnen to Carlisle in January 1914. After interviewing students, faculty and staff, Linnen reported how problems existed in virtually every department on campus due to what he saw as a lack of concern and oversight by Friedman. This investigation also found that the athletic director, Glenn "Pop" Warner, exercised so much influence over Friedman and the school that football and other sports

This circa 1913 snapshot shows Coach Glenn "Pop" Warner on the football field with his team at the Carlisle Indian Industrial School. The photograph was taken by Louis Hathaway, a teacher and disciplinarian at the school.

became more important than teaching the students. The school band and elaborate commencement exercises also ranked high on the priority list of what really mattered to the administration.

"Everything was done for advertisement, show and glitter," Principal Whitwell told Linnen, "all at the sacrifice of the schooling, farming, gardening, dairying, trades and industrial teaching...[e]verything was made to be subservient to athletics and football." As a result, few students became proficient in the trades, and there was almost a total lack of agricultural training. Male students assigned to work on a farm, a garden or in dairy were made to believe it was punishment. Some trades were completely abandoned, even though those courses were still mentioned in catalogues and other promotional material. It appeared as though the Carlisle Indian Industrial School had lost its way. This created the need for reform that Lipps mentioned in his letter to Hutchinson.

This greater emphasis on sports also manifested itself as a special privilege afforded to student athletes. They had better housing and clothing and were given gifts of watches, medals, suits and money. While classmates complained of poor-quality food and not having enough to eat, student athletes were treated to a special diet, a separate cook and their own training table in the dining hall. Naturally, this led to jealousy among the non-athletic students. Even the table settings were inadequate for the needs of most students. Linnen documented cases where students had to wait until their neighbor at the table was done with his or her knife before they could borrow it to cut their meat. There were even times when two students drank out of the same cup. This neglect extended to the living quarters, where non-athletes lacked blankets and had to sleep on old, worn-out mattresses.

The staff was not exempt from this inequality. Linnen noted how Warner received an annual salary of $4,000 (the modern equivalent of about $86,000) for what amounted to only three months of work. It was reported that Warner cut branches of school athletics he was not skilled at coaching, such as baseball and basketball. For years, he lived in government housing with heat and electricity already paid for. Meanwhile, instructors in the trades and industrial departments were paid $700 to $900 per year and had to rent places in town. They had to pay for all of their utilities, as well as daily trolley rides to and from the Indian school.

Student athletes complained how Warner cussed out players and came down hard on anyone who dared to voice their opinion. They accused Warner of loitering in hotel lobbies, selling complimentary away game tickets that were meant for school patrons and allegedly pocketing the cash. There

This image from a 1910 postcard shows students in the dining room of the Carlisle Indian Industrial School.

was even speculation Warner used the football team for gambling. Linnen recommended the school disregard the non-binding contract Warner had with Friedman and dismiss the athletic director in the best interests of the school. In a *Sentinel* article, Warner had this to say in his own defense:

> *Inspector Linnen made a vicious and malicious report against me as he did against every employee of the school who maintained their loyalty to the superintendent. He threatened to put me out of business if I did not cease supporting Mr. Friedman and when he found his threats did not deter me from doing what my duty prompted me, he did everything he could to endeavor to discredit me...*
>
> *His adverse report on me is not sustained by evidence and is a result simply of personal animosity and spite because I had the moral courage to oppose his farcical and one-sided investigation.*

To his credit, Warner was known as the "Great Originator" because he introduced many innovations to college football, including the three-point stance, numbering players' jerseys and the use of shoulder and thigh pads. He made the Carlisle Indian School one of the most well-trained football teams in the country. His athletes routinely challenged and defeated the likes of Pitt, Penn State, Harvard and Army on the gridiron. What's more, Coach Warner had defenders in the Carlisle community, as demonstrated by the following excerpts from a column published in the May 25, 1914 edition of the *Sentinel*:

> *On the football field at practice, on football trips to the cities, or at his home or office at the school, he has always been the same—a superior coach, a conservative business manager and a good leader for the Indian boys...*
>
> *Twelve years of successful athletic work are not to be overturned in a day by the alleged discovery of isolated facts which do not square with his career.*

Public opinion aside, the Indian boys on the football team took a leading role in the student rebellion by circulating a petition demanding that an investigation be made of the school. Over two hundred students signed the document, which claimed that school officials were expelling classmates who dared to criticize or challenge the administration. But according to Linnen's inspection report, nothing caused greater student unrest than the handling of the athletic fund. The Carlisle Indian School Athletic Association provided oversight of this fund and had Friedman and Warner listed as officers on both its articles of incorporation and its executive committee.

In reviewing the fund, Linnen found the books were properly kept and that some of the money was put to a "very good and worthy purpose." This included the purchase of construction materials to build the printing office, the firehouse and the business department of the academic building. However, Linnen also found evidence that "a large amount [of money] has been improperly used and [that] various interested parties have been subsidized."

There were payments to Friedman to cover hotel bills, trip expenses and theater tickets, as well as loans made to football players with little expectation of repayment. There was also evidence to suggest that two local newspaper correspondents were on the take to write favorable stories on Indian school athletics at the instigation of Warner. The fund even supplied the cameras for these journalists to use. Payouts were also made to the police chief, sheriff and

Superintendent Moses Friedman.

detectives to cover the arrest of troublesome students. While it was proper for this fund to cover expenses for away games, no subsidy was extended to non-athletic students, who had to pay for their own lodging and transportation—often causing great hardship to them and their families.

During his investigation, Linnen interviewed chief clerk Siceni Nori, who claimed he was ordered by Friedman to prepare false government travel vouchers, knowing at the time that the superintendent was also using mileage paid for by the athletic fund. There were also allegations that Friedman had ordered Nori to destroy government receipts and papers to conceal evidence of wrongdoing.

Not everyone was against the embattled superintendent. The following excerpts from an editorial published in the the *Carlisle Herald* voiced support for Friedman and concerns over the implications of the congressional inquiry:

> *The present investigation might develop into a pretext…a false fabric for the removal of the school from Carlisle. If this should culminate, the blame would be justly placed on Carlisle residents for it is on complaints based on selfish motives that have caused the present situation. Friedman is held at the highest esteem. He has been energetic in broadening the curriculum of the school and extending its practical courses by adopting several new and valuable ideas.*

In response to such speculation, U.S. senator Joseph Robinson tried to reassure Carlisle residents that there were no plans to remove the school. As chairman of the Joint Committee on Indian Affairs, he explained how the goal of the investigation was to probe the management practices at this school. This was being done in response to allegations of lax discipline, unjust expulsion of students, misrepresentations of the school to the public, unsanitary conditions and lack of adequate food. In early February 1914, committee members visited the Carlisle campus to convene hearings and receive testimony from students, staff, teachers and community members. On February 13, newspapers reported how Commissioner Sells suspended Friedman pending further investigation of the school. Friedman later resigned.

Friedman was outspoken in his defense. He blamed Democrats under the Wilson administration for orchestrating the uproar at the school as part of a conspiracy to oust as many Republicans as possible from office. Friedman also denied allegations he had ordered Nori to destroy evidence.

In July 1914, the federal government offered Friedman immunity on the grounds the prosecution lacked sufficient evidence to go to trial and had ruled that the statute of limitations had expired on many of the alleged crimes. Friedman fired back:

> *I want this inquiry to go on until...my reputation is vindicated and the conditions which drove me to resign have been shown to be the result of a carefully planned persecution at the hands of the Bureau of Indian Affairs under commissioner Sells.*
>
> *As for the accusations of irregularities in the finances of the school, there is not one transaction in which I could not render an account. That the testimony of Nori...should have been accepted shows the malignance of the attack upon me. During my incumbency, I handled $2 million of the school's funds. My accounts show that not one penny of it was misappropriated.*
>
> *All that I have in the world is my character. I cannot suffer this injustice, which seeks relentlessly to ruin me, to go on. I have absolutely nothing to fear from the most searching inquiry that can be brought to bear on the matter. I welcome it.*

Ultimately, the embezzlement charges against Friedman were dismissed, and he was vindicated through an appointment to another federal position. This left Lipps and his promises of reform behind, but there was little he could do as chief administrator to stop the decline of the Carlisle school. Times had changed. More non-reservation schools had been established in the West. Indian children no longer had to travel east to get an education, and leaders in Washington, D.C., thought it made more sense economically to encourage enrollment in the western schools. Enrollment at Carlisle dwindled rapidly after the congressional investigation.

In the end, the school was closed by the War Department, which exercised its right to revoke the transfer of Carlisle Barracks to the Department of the Interior. This was done by necessity to care for wounded World War I veterans returning from Europe. During the summer of 1918, all remaining Carlisle students were sent home or to other non-reservation schools throughout the country. On September 1, 1918, the Carlisle Indian Industrial School ceased to exist and became United States Army Base Hospital Number 31.

Part III

Lurid Legends

It is often said that homeownership and being your own boss are all just part of the American dream. But this can turn surreal if the family-run business happens to be a whorehouse. For nearly a century, mother Cora Andrews and daughter Bessie Jones functioned as madams in a back alley of Carlisle. While their girls sold sexual favors to regular customers, other women around town were being terrorized by a fiend with loose ties to a monster that once stalked the streets of London's East End. His weapon of choice was the warm embrace, not the cold steel of his British cousin. But this section begins with a much earlier tale about a violent drunk and restless spirit, whose legacy continues on as a crude example of quality folk art.

Hanger-On

Rowdy Old Schimmel

The lonely old man with the sad, droopy face bowed down to temptation. He let his pride in his work turn into a rage that could not be contained. Wilhelm Schimmel entered the contest, confident that his carving of the Garden of Eden would win him the blue ribbon at the annual Carlisle fair. It was a different kind of sculpture for the tramp artist—one that spoke to generations of Bavarian peasants. The scene measured ten inches square, with a nine-inch-high tree in the center. Coiled around the trunk was a serpent offering Adam the proverbial apple. But the judges rejected Schimmel's work for that of others, causing him to let loose a flood of German curses upon their heads. In Schimmel, anger and artistry came together in a big, ugly frame, topped by thinning hair and wrapped in a rumpled-up jacket.

No one really knows the details of his life before he showed up in the Cumberland Valley just after the Civil War. There was speculation Schimmel left his native Germany because he was heartbroken over the death of his wife, on the run as a fugitive from military service, escaping an unhappy love affair or facing charges of murder. Whatever his motives, he kept them secret and made very few friends. His rowdy behavior when drunk became the stuff of legend. In life, Schimmel was a regular in the taverns of Carlisle, trading his carvings for pints of whiskey. A restless spirit, he wandered the countryside along the Conodoguinet Creek between Newburg and Carlisle, and he always had with him his trusty penknife and one or more blocks of pine wood—for what made Schimmel famous were his carvings. More than a century has passed since his death from stomach

Wilhelm Schimmel, circa 1875.

cancer and burial in a pauper's grave in 1890. The rowdy old drunk has since attained status he never knew in life and probably never sought. His carvings grace the halls of fine museums worldwide and can sell for tens of thousands of dollars at auction.

Schimmel is regarded as an important figure in American woodcarving. His work today is highly recognized and greatly revered, but in life, his carvings were simple gifts or objects he bartered to support his drinking habit and transient lifestyle. At best, they were traded for only a few pennies and put on humble display on the mantels of local homes and on shelves in local taverns.

Newspaper accounts and stories of his life paint us a portrait of a violent drunk when under the influence and a harmless, inoffensive man when sober. On February 15, 1883, the *Evening Sentinel* described Schimmel as a "hanger on" at the county jail and poorhouse and as a man who seemed to bear a charmed life in the Carlisle area: "He has been the hero of numberless fights and although the snows of nearly four-score winters have fallen on his head, his vigor has not abated and his strength is something marvelous." The article's describing Schimmel as having fourscore years would put him close to eighty, but poorhouse records would later document his birth year as 1817, making him sixty-six at the time the article was published.

On May 7, 1869, Schimmel walked into the office of the Delancey and Shrom lumberyard in Carlisle, highly intoxicated and covered in mud. Just as he was about to relax on Shrom's chair, Schimmel was ordered to sit down on a bench. As Shrom went upstairs to attend to business, John Goodyear ordered the old carver to leave. The *Carlisle Herald* reported how Shrom heard a scuffle downstairs and called out to Goodyear, asking if he needed any help tossing the old drunk out of the office. Just as Goodyear replied "No," Schimmel got the best of him and forced Goodyear to make a hasty retreat.

At that point, Shrom rushed downstairs to find Schimmel, a club in hand, breaking apart the furniture and overturning the red hot stove. The *Herald* reported how Shrom and Goodyear rallied, each grabbing a club before going after Schimmel. They knocked the old man down two or three times before forcing him to leave. They backed off, thinking their troubles were over, but the situation was about to get worse. Schimmel attacked John Hays, a lumberyard employee, as he was approaching the yard. Hays knocked Schimmel down a few times with his fist but found the old man to be too powerful. Hays then retreated, followed closely by Schimmel, who started to throw stones at both the employee and the lumberyard office. The three men then went after Schimmel with stones of their own and subdued the old man, who later entered a guilty plea to an assault charge and served one year in county jail.

Almost fourteen years later, on February 14, 1883, Schimmel entered the Mansion House Hotel on the southwest corner of West High and South Pitt Streets in Carlisle. He sat himself down and dozed off before he was awakened by the proprietor, who asked him to leave. Schimmel refused and instead "launched a spirited attack against those around him," according to the *Herald*. As police were being called to the scene, the old drunk left the building but was observed minutes later calmly walking down North Hanover Street on his way to a local bar. After resisting arrest, Schimmel was remanded to jail for ten days before being released once again.

Six months later, on August 1, 1883, Schimmel got into a "wordy war" with a fellow German while waiting for the evening train at the Cumberland Valley Railroad depot next door to the hotel. The verbal exchange developed into a full-blown cane fight. "Blows and thrusts were clearly given and received, but old age and whiskey weakened the effect," the *Sentinel* reported. "Neither of them was badly hurt." While the cause of the fight was a total mystery, the newspaper labeled Schimmel the aggressor. Both men would later board the westbound train, but they continued to swear at each other in German and shake their canes in a threatening manner.

A ride on the westbound train from Carlisle on May 21, 1882, nearly proved fatal for Schimmel. The train blew its whistle to alert passengers that it was about one mile from the station house at Greason. Thinking that he had arrived at his destination, an intoxicated Schimmel walked out of the car and off the platform while the train was still running at full speed in the vicinity of Kerrsville. As the train pulled into the Greason station, the train conductor was alerted to what had happened, and he ordered the train to reverse course to where Schimmel lay injured. The old man was loaded onto the baggage car of the 6:30 p.m. eastbound train to Carlisle. He was then

This 1870 photograph by A.A. Line shows the Mansion House Hotel and the Cumberland Valley Railroad Station, both of which were scenes of rowdiness perpetrated by Wilhelm Schimmel.

transported to the county poorhouse, where he received medical treatment for over a month for head and eye injuries.

When he wasn't in jail or in the county poorhouse, Schimmel would wander the countryside, staying with families of mostly German descent. Greason was located near where the Greider family operated a gristmill along what is now Creek Road, north of Plainfield in West Pennsboro Township. Schimmel would sleep in the loft of their washhouse and sit for hours by the covered bridge, singing songs in his native German as he carved figures from pine wood. The strange man attracted neighborhood children who were intrigued by what he was doing, many even trying to imitate him. One boy became so adept at the craft that his carvings are almost as sought after as his mentor's, even though his output was considerably less. Sources say Aaron Mountz turned out fewer than fifty pieces in his lifetime compared to the hundreds carved by Schimmel.

The old man developed such a close bond with these children that some of their parents trusted Schimmel to babysit them while they were running errands in town. Schimmel would stay up to a week at a time with the Hensel family of Newburg, Hopewell Township. They had a "bummer" room in their summer kitchen loft that they made available to tramps in exchange for a day's labor. One night in 1884, Schimmel issued a challenge to John Hensel Jr., who was only four or five years old at the time. "If you kiss the hired girl," he said, "I will make you something." Sure enough, the boy climbed onto the girl's lap and gave her a kiss. Schimmel kept his promise and gave the young lad one of his signature eagles.

Not everything about country living went well for Schimmel, as illustrated by two incidents reported near Greider's bridge. On July 15, 1873, the carver became so enraged by something, he struck a boy with his fist and threatened to hit the mother with a stick. Witnesses for the prosecution included a relative of Samuel Bloser, a local cabinetmaker and undertaker, who routinely supplied the old carver with scrap wood. For his crime, Schimmel was taken to jail and held on a $100 bail. The second incident took place on February 28, 1879, during a public sale in nearby Frankford Township. Schimmel used an axe to attack a man named Nickey, who acted in self-defense by hitting the old drunk on the head with a stone. Initial press reports claimed that Schimmel had died from injuries that had knocked him unconscious.

Finally in mid-May 1890, Schimmel took sick and was transported (despite his protests) to the poorhouse in the back of a wagon belonging to a friend, a German butcher named Hoffress. The old carver would die three months later on August 3 at the reported age of seventy-three. Penniless, he was buried three days later in an unmarked grave on what is now the campus of the Claremont Nursing and Rehabilitation Center in Middlesex Township. His reputation in life was such that local newspapers published his obituary—a rare practice for a tramp. Thirty-seven years later, in 1927, a two-day sell was held, which included ten Schimmel carvings. This was believed to be the first time his work was widely advertised and publicly sold. The first major exhibition of his work was held at Colonial Williamsburg in 1965, showcasing eighty-three Schimmel carvings.

This wood carving of an eagle by Wilhelm Schimmel is in the collection of the Cumberland County Historical Society.

Historians estimate his output to be between 1,000 and 1,500 carvings, of which about 300 to 400 exist today. Most of his work consists of birds and animal figures, such as eagles, roosters, dogs, squirrels and parrots. Schimmel was especially fond of eagles, patterning them after the European Hapsburgian emblem instead of the American bald eagle. Nearly one hundred of his eagles survive today, from pocket-sized to those with a wingspan of over two feet. It appears that Schimmel had some marketing savvy in that he produced popular subjects multiple times but crafted each individual piece so that no two were exactly alike. His eagle motif fit in well with the social and economic climate of post–Civil War America. In May 2012, a Schimmel eagle was listed on an antiques price list at $234,000.

The Index of American Design describes his carvings as technically crude, but they are still treasured as lively portrayals of their subjects. For larger subjects, he would carve separate pieces of wood, which were then glued together or held in place by a pin, suggesting Schimmel had some training earlier in life. The strokes were made with a quick hand using a penknife on scrap wood salvaged from barn raisings, sawmills and carpentry shops throughout the Cumberland Valley. Once a piece was finished, Schimmel would coat it with a layer of gesso and then polychrome paint, predominately in red, black, yellow or green. The carvings were meant to fit a space on a mantel or a corner cupboard. Schimmel would often carry around a basket full of carvings to sell on Carlisle streets for ten cents or a quarter each.

There are no known pieces signed by him because his signature meant little to Schimmel and to the people receiving his carvings. They knew it was his work by his reputation. Schimmel carvings have been displayed at the National Gallery of Art in Washington, D.C., the Boston Museum of Fine Art, the Philadelphia Museum of Art and the Metropolitan Museum of Art in New York City. At thirty-two pieces, the collection at the Cumberland County Historical Society is believed to be among the largest in the United States.

A Warm Reception

The Jack the Hugger Affair

When asked why he was wearing women's clothing, the seventy-nine-year-old cross-dresser explained that his wife had died and left him the garments, so he thought he should wear them. His taste in fashion confirmed police suspicions that they had just arrested the "Jack the Hugger" who had been frightening women and girls all over Carlisle for the past two months. It was obvious the coal-black kid gloves, buttoned-down black shoes and black hat with a veil concealed a man who suffered "a mental aberration," the *Evening Sentinel* reported. The poor, wretched soul actually believed he had done no harm and had promised authorities he would stop wearing ladies' outfits.

It was just after 7:30 a.m. on October 12, 1925, and a crowd of about one hundred men and boys was following a police officer down West High Street. The patrolman was escorting the "Jack" he had just arrested near the corner of West Street. Authorities believed this was the man suspected of forcing his affection upon many an unwilling and unreceptive female. The night before, this fiend in drag scared a woman of the First Ward, leading the *Sentinel* to speculate that "had he been caught, he would have been handled roughly." Even Burgess Jasper Alexander warned the poor wretch of the consequences of going out at night dressed as a woman. Anything could happen in Carlisle.

No name was ever given for the old man except "Jack the Hugger," a generic term newspapers used at that time to describe any man who accosted women on the street. Aside from his dress and mental state, details were sketchy on the widower. He was a white male living in the Third

Ward in what is today the southwest section of town. Just as one "Jack" was apprehended, another was on the loose; police were searching for a taller man wearing puttees who was also accused of scaring women and girls. But these were not the only reports from Carlisle of stalkers tagged with the same moniker that was probably derived from Jack the Ripper, the mysterious figure behind one of the most infamous series of unsolved murders in crime history.

The year before, on October 23, 1924, the *Sentinel* reported that a "Jack the Hugger" had frightened a West Louther Street woman who "screamed loud and long." The same article mentioned how this particular hugger grabbed the wrists of a West Pomfret Street woman after she answered her doorbell. In that case, the woman "kicked him severely out on the pavement," the newspaper reported. Seven years earlier, on April 6, 1917, the *Sentinel* demanded local police exert every effort possible to locate and severely punish Carlisle's "Jack the Hugger," who roamed the streets in early fall 1916 and terrorized women by embracing them. One lady on Lincoln Street and another on Louther Street were nearly scared to death when this man put his arms around them and squeezed hard.

The 1917 article went on to report a dramatic intervention by a relative. As the story goes, a young woman was unlocking the door to her Pitt Street home around ten o'clock one evening when a Jack grabbed and hugged her tight. The lady screamed, prompting family members to rush to her side and investigate. Her brother-in-law chased the hugger down Pitt Street, until the perpetrator turned on Church Avenue toward the old county courthouse. Witnesses described him as the same man who had terrorized women the previous fall, a man with a dark complexion wearing a hat and knee breeches. "A warm reception awaits him when he is caught," the *Sentinel* reported.

Yet Carlisle was not alone. A quick online search for "Jack the Hugger" cases turned up references to similar crimes all over the United States, starting at around 1890 and continuing into the mid- to late 1920s. An October 1890 article from the *Logan Journal* in Utah confirmed the "Jack the Hugger" copycat crimes corresponded with the sensation generated by the Ripper murders in London of 1888. The writer for the *Journal* had this to say in an editorial entitled "How Many Jacks?": "How many Jacks are we to have? Since the name Jack through the atrocities of the Ripper has become a synonym for much of what is horrible, there have developed a succession of other Jacks. That is not surprising when we contemplate the sheep following instincts of the human race, but which is nauseating nevertheless."

The *Journal* writer mentioned shortly after the Ripper murders made international news that "a creature in one of the eastern cities made himself notorious" by throwing ink on the clothing of women who passed him on the street. He was immediately labeled "Jack the Ink Slinger." This was followed by the case of a "semi-demented fellow with a passion for tobacco chewing" who spat on ladies' dresses. He became known as "Jack the Spitter." Then came the first newspaper reports of an individual who "became very numerous in certain quarters" because of his conduct of either kissing or hugging nearly every pretty girl he came across. "He was variously dubbed 'Jack the Kisser' or 'Jack the Hugger' according to the strong impression he left on the fair victim," the *Journal* reported. It appeared this editorial came out of a recent and disturbing turn of events: "Now comes a fellow with a weakness for the soft tresses of hair that are a crown of glory to so many women. He must have them so he clips them cleanly off and makes way with them. He is called 'Jack the Haircutter.' This thing has only really fairly started."

Moral Plague Spot

The House of Cora

They were the uninvited guests of a chicken and waffle dinner hosted by one of Carlisle's most notorious madams. When a police officer knocked on the whorehouse door, a curious voice from an upstairs window asked, "What's going on?" It was 11:00 p.m. on Saturday, November 3, 1917, and authorities were anxious to get the raid over with. They shouted back their ultimatum: "Unlock the door or we will force it open!" Someone inside the Locust Avenue brothel obeyed the order, and the cops rushed in through the front and back doors only to find "house guests" and "inmates" sitting around the kitchen table enjoying a late-night supper.

Officers arrested three black women—the madam, named Cora Andrews, and her daughters, Bessie Jones and Marion Gibson. They also took into custody a white girl named Gay Newman, four johns who happened to be soldiers from Gettysburg, over one hundred bottles of beer and some whiskey. In its coverage, the *Sentinel* newspaper viewed this latest development with a degree of cautious optimism:

> *What effect the recent raid and arrests will have on the morals of the community remains to be seen. All summer the place has been frequented by soldiers from Gettysburg, but nothing officially was done to suppress the joint by the local authorities...It is stated visitors to the notorious resort were so frequent at times that men were lined up outside waiting to enter. District Attorney [George] Lloyd, his assistant and the officers are receiving praise from every decent citizen today in the hope, for the sake of the town, the Andrews place has been eradicated forever*

and that proper punishment that fits the crimes charged will be meted out to all guilty parties.

Alas, forever was not meant to be. While the soldiers were later released, Cora Andrews pled guilty in early December to one count of keeping a bawdyhouse. She was sentenced to six months in Cumberland County Jail and ordered to pay a $250 fine. While Newman and Gibson also pled guilty, they were jailed until they could pay a $25 fine. There was no mention of Bessie Jones in the 1917 court docket.

On March 21, 1918, Judge Sylvester B. Sadler granted Cora Andrews parole into the custody of a county probation officer, citing her poor health and time served in jail since November as his reasons for releasing her early. "If it shall be made to appear the defendant is guilty of any further misbehavior, a bench warrant will be issued," Sadler warned Andrews. Three months later, on June 29, the same judge issued a bench warrant for her arrest on charges that she resumed operating a house "in a disorderly manner so as to make necessary the interference by police." Her parole was revoked. Authorities arrested her later that day, and she was ordered to serve out the rest of her December sentence.

November 1917 was not the first or last time Andrews "fell into the clutches of the law," as the *Sentinel* reported after the raid. Her involvement in prostitution is well documented. County docket books have entries on this madam going back to 1886 when, on April 12 of that year, a jury found Andrews guilty of keeping a disorderly house and keeping a bawdyhouse. She was sentenced to eighteen months in county jail and ordered to pay a $50 fine. Three years later, in April 1889, Andrews pled guilty to similar charges and was sentenced to at least ten days in jail, plus whatever time was necessary for her to pay the costs of prosecution. She was then released on her own recognizance on the condition that she pay $100 in security and "abide by the laws of the Commonwealth and keep the law toward all the good citizens for a period of eighteen months," the docket entry reads. But that did not last. In 1894, Cora Andrews again pled guilty to the exact same charges and was sentenced to nine months in county jail.

Black's Law Dictionary, Seventh Edition, defines a "disorderly house" as a dwelling where people carry on activities that are a nuisance to the neighborhood. The definition quoted the text "Criminal Law" by Rollin M. Perkins and Ronald N. Boyce:

The keeping of one type of disorderly house—the bawdy house—is punishable because it violates the social interests in maintaining proper standards of morality and decency…Any house in which disorderly persons are permitted to congregate, and to disturb the tranquility of the neighborhood by fighting, quarrelling, swearing and any other type of disorder, is a disorderly house.

Cora Andrews continued to be a thorn to the Carlisle community. In the spring of 1902, former Dickinson College president George Reed filed charges against the madam in an attempt to shut down her operation. On May 15, 1902, she pled guilty to separate counts of keeping a bawdyhouse and keeping a disorderly house. She was released on her own recognizance on the condition that she pay the costs of prosecution and $300 in security, as well as refrain from further operating a whorehouse. Three months later, on August 12, 1902, police raided her property again and brought Andrews before the court for breach of recognizance. She was ordered confined to the county jail, only to be released after she paid the costs of prosecution and $600 in "approved security," according to the court docket. Less than nine years later on May 2, 1911, the *Sentinel* reported that Andrews and two other women were brought before a federal grand jury in Harrisburg on charges that they had furnished liquor to Carlisle Indian School students. The following day, a jury found Andrews guilty and a federal judge ordered her to serve two months in Cumberland County Jail and pay a $100 fine plus the costs of prosecution. That was the maximum sentence under the law for that offense. The judge ordered Andrews confined until all the costs were fully paid off.

Andrews appeared in court cradling a child in her arms and was accompanied by other children. The jury recommended mercy. When asked if she had anything to say, Andrews replied that she only had a few dollars, but both the judge and the newspaper saw this as a ploy to avoid paying fines and costs. In a May 3, 1911 article, the *Sentinel* explained how federal law bars prisoners from pleading insolvency to dodge payments. Instead, fines and costs must either be paid directly or served out as time in jail at a rate of one dollar per day. In the case of Andrews, this meant confinement of six months to a year in the county jail. In handing down his sentence, the judge said the Indians had been sent to Carlisle to be protected and that he would help accomplish that mission.

Twelve years later, on May 19, 1923, the *Sentinel* made reference to a case from 1920, where Andrews pled guilty to keeping a bawdyhouse and was ordered to pay costs and enter recognizance. It was reported how, in August 1920, she broke her recognizance and was held under a $600 bond to appear at court in September, where she was sentenced to pay a $50 fine and to spend a year in jail. This part of her criminal record came up in 1923 because District Attorney Merrill Hummel wanted to show the court that Andrews was "a notorious colored woman of Carlisle." She was up for sentencing after a jury on May 14, 1923, convicted her of keeping a bawdyhouse. While the *Sentinel* did not report on the testimony from the one-day trial, it had a complete story on the sentencing that included the following excerpt:

> *Former District Attorney John M. Rhey, attorney for the Law and Order Society, argued that Andrews had for years persisted in defying the law with a most detrimental effect on the moral and physical welfare of the community. In other words, he said, her house was a moral plague spot in the community for years….Notwithstanding her age, the law should be allowed to take its course and a substantial sentence should be imposed.*

In asking for clemency, defense attorney Herman Berg stated his client was a seventy-year-old woman who was nearly blind and in poor health. He thought it heartless and cruel that prosecutors should ask for a substantial sentence. Berg also thought her reputation should have no relevance in the case currently before the court. But Rhey argued it would be silly for the court not to take her reputation into consideration as a vital element in the case. Judge Edward W. Biddle agreed with the jury verdict, stating there was plenty of evidence to prove her guilt beyond her reputation. "The age of the woman was not an excuse," the judge ruled. He then sentenced her to thirteen months in county jail plus whatever time was necessary beyond that for her to pay a total of $684 in fines and costs.

Shortly after her thirteen months were up, the attorney for Andrews filed a petition asking the court to grant her release from jail for non-payment of fines and costs. The docket entry mentions how Andrews was "broken in health" and "under the constant care of a physician." "The petitioner was without funds, has no income and can earn no money being solely dependent on her children for support," the docket reads.

On September 18, 1924, Andrews filed a complete listing of her property as further proof she was indigent and should be released without further delay under the state insolvency laws. The county commissioners granted her request, and she was discharged from the county jail. There is no further

The Andrews family burial plot at Union Cemetery in Carlisle. *Photo by Joseph David Cress.*

listing for Cora Andrews in the court docket. As the story goes, she turned the operation of the whorehouse over to her daughter, Bessie Jones. Her tombstone in Union Cemetery reads "Cora J. Andrews, 1867 to 1945" even though census data lists her as being two months old in 1860.

The whorehouse is said to date back to the Civil War, when Cora's mother, Jane Andrews, a former slave and camp follower, arrived in Carlisle in June 1863 with the Confederate forces that had occupied the town. As the story goes, when the soldiers left for Gettysburg, Jane, seeing a business opportunity in Carlisle, stayed behind and opened a brothel. One legend tied to Jane was that her whorehouse allegedly catered to Confederate troops on certain days of the week and to Union troops on the other days. While this makes for colorful reading, this is probably false.

For one thing, data from the 1860 census shows that Jane Andrews was already in Carlisle before the war even began. She was listed as a twenty-nine-year-old black woman who was born in Maryland. Illiterate, she was employed as a cook and had three children at home at the time of the census—all of whom were listed as being born in Pennsylvania. If this information is accurate, Jane had to have been in the Keystone State in

Close-up of the tombstone of Cora Andrews, a longtime madam in Carlisle. *Photo by Joseph David Cress.*

1854, because Charles, her oldest son, was listed as being six years old at the time of the 1860 census. Her two other children were two-year-old David and two-month-old Cora.

It is said that Jane operated the whorehouse for about forty years before turning the operation over to Cora sometime around the turn of the century. However, court documents suggest that it was Cora alone who operated a whorehouse and that Jane may not have been involved in prostitution at all. While there are criminal court docket entries for Cora Andrews going back as far as 1886, there is nothing at all listed in the docket books under Jane Andrews going back to before the Civil War. In the opinion of the author, this could mean several things: one, Jane was never a madam; two, her name is listed under an alias; three, the authorities were either corrupt or tolerated her whorehouse; four, Jane was so good at concealing her operation that she escaped notice and was never caught. True or false, the story of Jane Andrews has endured for generations.

A Carlisle Institution

Madam Bessie Jones

There was something about the handsome young john that suggested a trap. The money he used to pay for sex was separate from other cash in his pocket. He was good-looking, whereas most of the clientele were homely middle-aged men. But the dead giveaway for Katherine "Kit" Harrison was how the man backed away slightly when she first approached him with a basin full of warm, soapy water. It was, after all, standard procedure for working girls employed at Bessie's Place to wash and dry each client before starting a new transaction.

Harrison only caught on to the subtle clues after the undercover state trooper got up from the bed before anything could happen and retrieved the badge he had hidden in his shoe. Showing her proof he was a police officer only scared the prostitute half to death. "She was so frightened she might have fallen out through the window," Detective Sergeant Robert Smith wrote later in his arrest report. "He kept her from falling by holding her by the arm until she could recover her composure."

It was about 9:00 p.m. on Thursday, June 27, 1963, when trooper Matthew Hunt first stepped onto the porch of Carlisle's most notorious whorehouse. From a distance, the dwelling at 20 East Locust Street looked fairly ordinary—just a two-and-a-half-story frame building covered with gray siding and trimmed in green. But for decades, this address was a blight for some, a delight for others, but it eventually became the scene of first an arson investigation and then an unsolved murder case. But that was in the future. For Hunt, getting in was part of the mission to raid the brothel and arrest its most famous resident, madam Bessie Jane Jones.

This May 1972 photograph by James Steinmetz shows the front porch of Bessie's Place, the notorious whorehouse that once stood at 20 East Locust Street. It is now part of a parking lot.

The record is unclear as to whether Hunt rang the doorbell or knocked. As expected, Jones answered, peering out into the night at the stranger on her porch. Police knew ahead of time that it was customary for the old black woman to question each guest she was unfamiliar with. Scrutiny was necessary to filter out the riffraff and the college students. They were not welcome. Neither were black or Hispanic males. As her attorney, Hyman Goldstein, explained to a judge in 1959, Bessie provided the community with a much-needed service by catering only to high-class white men. Hers was a Carlisle institution on par with Molly Pitcher, Jim Thorpe, Dickinson College and Dickinson School of Law, Goldstein declared.

No mention was made in Smith's arrest report of what Hunt had said to Jones to convince the savvy businesswoman to allow him entry into the whorehouse. Once inside, Hunt saw two men emerge from a backroom. They were led out the front door by Jones, who first looked both ways up the alley to make sure no one was watching. Before they left, Jones remarked how she was worried about them. She hadn't seen them in weeks and had missed their patronage.

Hunt was then approached by a light-skinned black woman named Constance Morris. She had red hair and was wearing black-and-white checkered shorts, a black blouse and long, dangling earrings. She asked if she could help, but Hunt said no. Upon her arrest, Morris told police she was not offended: Business was business and some johns preferred sex with a white woman. Besides, she had turned more tricks than Harrison since they both arrived at Bessie's Place that Sunday. The prostitutes explained how they had heard about the Carlisle whorehouse from other working girls who said the money was good. Operating independently, Morris and Harrison had contacted Jones and made arrangements to split their earnings fifty-fifty with the old madam.

The night of the raid, Harrison approached Hunt and nodded her head toward the stairs. She had her black hair in a ponytail and was wearing a green print blouse and orange shorts. Once upstairs, she asked what she could do for him. Posing as a john, Hunt responded, "What do you think I am here for?" She replied, "Well, honey, a lot of guys want it different ways." She then outlined all the options with the corresponding price list. He made a selection and paid her ten dollars in marked bills. Police later recovered the money as evidence, along with the washbasin, soap, paper napkins used for drying and "trick books," which documented the sex acts performed and the money taken in since the girls first arrived for their two-week stint at the whorehouse. It was routine for Jones to cycle girls through the brothel, keeping them confined to the premises so they could not mingle with the townsfolk. The wise old madam was careful to turn certain local men away because of their tendency to talk too much.

After being paid, Harrison told Hunt to undress and relax while she went downstairs to hand the money over to Jones, who kept it in a black pocketbook in the kitchen. On her way back, Harrison stopped at the bathroom to draw a basin of water. Sex acts were performed in two bedrooms, one on the second floor and one in the attic. Depending on how busy they were, the prostitutes alternated between the two rooms but shared the bathroom. Harrison was all set to service a john who wanted half-and-half oral and straight sex, only to discover that her customer was a police officer. After calming her down, Hunt got dressed, went downstairs and gave the pre-arranged signal that summoned other officers to the scene.

The 9:30 p.m. raid on Bessie's Place capped a year-long investigation that started in early June 1962 when police received word that Jones was again operating a whorehouse from her Locust Street address. All three women were arrested and pled guilty to the charges. Harrison and Morris were sentenced to sixty days in jail and ordered to pay $100 fines. Jones was sentenced to six months in county prison and ordered to pay a $500 fine. This was nothing new for Jones, a repeat offender who took over the family enterprise from her mother, Cora Andrews.

Jones was first arrested as a madam in 1939 and was sentenced that August to two years in county prison. That jail term was later suspended for equal time on probation. On May 9, 1941, seven people were arrested in a raid on the Locust Street address by Carlisle police and Liquor Control Board (LCB) agents. Seven quarts of whiskey, a quart of gin and three cases of beer were confiscated. Jones was charged with keeping a disorderly house and selling liquor without a license. She pled no contest and was sentenced to sixty days to six months in jail.

All was quiet until March 26, 1959, when authorities again raided the property. This time, they caught two prostitutes having sex with customers in the upstairs bedrooms. Seven other men were turned away by state troopers processing the scene. Both girls were taken into custody along with Jones, who was also accused of selling beer by the bottle and whiskey by the shot for twenty-five cents apiece. LCB agents confiscated 2 bottles each of wine and whiskey and 102 bottles of beer. Rather than have it go to waste, a local judge ordered the alcohol be turned over to the county nursing home for hospital use. Jones was charged with operating a bawdyhouse and selling liquor without a license. She pled guilty that April and was ordered to pay a $500 fine and spend six months in jail, but Goldstein presented evidence showing that Jones was under treatment for various ailments and argued prolonged confinement would be detrimental to her health.

The son of a Russian immigrant, Goldstein achieved national renown as Bessie's defense attorney. He never denied that Jones was a madam. "I've defended and represented people in this community for more than five decades," Goldstein said. "I've had my share of characters who were bad apples. Bessie wasn't one of them. She wasn't too bright, but she was honest and she tried to do what she felt was right." Once, when Goldstein convinced the court to dismiss a rape charge against her nephew, an overjoyed Bessie rushed up to him and shouted, "Hymie, have one on the house." Another time, she entered his office just as a steel executive was leaving. Being polite, Goldstein introduced the man to the legendary madam, who blurted out, "I don't recall the name, but I remember the face." The man laughed.

Hyman Goldstein.

Those old enough remember Jones as a plump black woman who wore big floppy hats and too much makeup. She often used a cane when she walked downtown to the market, but many suspect this was more for show. Many local residents overlooked or tolerated her business, regarding her as both a kindly old madam who donated money to charity and as a benefactor to black families who struggled during the Depression. In sharp contrast, prostitutes employed by Bessie saw her as a cruel and cantankerous boss who never showed her appreciation.

Yet this madam was savvy enough to know not to mix black and white patrons together during a time of racial tensions or to allow college students entry, as the community would likely turn against her and accuse her of corrupting the morals of Carlisle's youth. Instead, her whorehouse catered mostly to white men in positions of power, including judges, generals, police chiefs and legislators. This may be one reason why she stayed in operation for decades.

Her downfall began in 1960, when the federal government charged Jones with five counts of income tax evasion for failing to file tax returns on $81,705 deposited in a Carlisle bank between 1954 and 1958. The Internal Revenue Service was also determining whether action was warranted for deposits as far back as 1940. Until the IRS contacted her in 1959, Jones never understood that everyone had to file a tax return, Goldstein told a judge.

In July 1961, IRS investigator James Mead testified in federal court that Jones had $191,000 in savings when the government first launched its probe of her bank records back in 1960. Mead added the bulk of her earnings came from the numbers game and horse racing in New York. U.S. judge Frederick Follmer sentenced Jones to one year in federal prison and five years probation but told her she may be eligible for parole given her age and physical condition. He also ordered Jones to divorce herself and her real estate from anything having to do with prostitution. Goldstein requested leniency on the grounds his client was ignorant of the tax law, but Follmer was convinced Jones was no financial neophyte and instead issued this stern rebuke as quoted by the *Sentinel*: "This woman has never done an honest day's work in her life and yet has managed to amass nearly $200,000. And all these arrests and times in prison…they apparently don't mean a thing to her as do the authorities over there in Carlisle."

Jones would spend the next eight months in a federal prison before being paroled for ill health. Her parole expired on July 10, 1962. In early June of that year, the state police began its year-long investigation of Bessie's Place after receiving word Jones was again operating a whorehouse. This resulted in the June 1963 raid mentioned earlier. That September, Jones was sentenced to six months in county jail but was paroled after six weeks after Goldstein submitted statements from two doctors who testified that prolonged confinement would be detrimental to her health.

Though free from county prison, Jones could not escape the wrath of a federal court judge, who was upset that she had violated probation by reestablishing her whorehouse. On October 10, 1963, Jones went before Follmer, who revoked her probation and sentenced her to three years in prison. He did this despite a plea from her defense that Jones suffered from severe arthritis and swelling of the limbs due to a heart condition. She also had poor hearing and vision.

"I thought I made myself pretty clear at that time," Follmer said. "Regardless of what her status may have been in the community, she was under the order from this court to desist from that sort of business…She knew well enough what I had in mind." The judge added that, while he respected the opinions of doctors, he felt the federal prison system was equipped to address Bessie's health problems. Bessie was three months into her prison sentence when firefighters responded to a fire at her vacant whorehouse just after 8:45 p.m. on Saturday, January 18, 1964. They were able to save the building, but the first floor was badly damaged.

Fire chief Ray Kelley called in the state police fire marshal after he noticed the whorehouse had been ransacked. Furniture and dresser drawers were strewn all over the floor. Police chief Ed Still ordered his men to pick up Frank Stackfield of 24 East Locust Street, figuring he may have knowledge about the fire. Police arrested not only Stackfield but also Beatrice Gibson, who lived at the same address. Officers found $5,600 in small bills on Stackfield and $520 on Gibson.

Upon questioning, Gibson broke down and confessed she had set the fire by pouring kerosene found in the basement over a sofa in a room on the first floor. She threw the fuel can into the outhouse. Gibson told police the fire was started after she, Stackfield and Ralph Conn stole money from the property. Meanwhile, Stackfield agreed to show police a third-floor closet where Jones had kept money stuffed in a pillowcase. The mass of bills totaled $48,606 and consisted of bill denominations from $5 to $100. The investigation led police to arrest a third man, Ralph Graham, who had $850 in his possession. Graham told officers he had known about the pillowcase for about two weeks before the burglary. The conspirators admitted to removing cash since January 10.

On March 24, 1964, Judge Dale Shughart sentenced Gibson to eleven to twenty-three months in county jail after she pled guilty to two counts of burglary and one count of arson. The others involved were given lesser sentences. Two years later, a federal judge determined that the IRS was entitled to $55,591 seized in the burglary arrests and confiscated from the pillowcase. This money was to be applied to the $174,163 in back taxes Jones owed the federal government. Bessie managed to stay out of trouble for two more years until the evening of June 29, 1968.

Acting on a tip, state police obtained a search warrant and organized yet another raid on the whorehouse. This time around, they had received word that Bessie's Place was catering to truck drivers using the interstate highway system that crisscrosses Cumberland County. Corporal Paul Petzar and Trooper Charles McBreen went to a local truck stop where they hailed a taxicab to go to 20 East Locust Street. Arriving at about 9:55 p.m., McBreen told Jones they had been sent there by truck drivers. The story worked, and the undercover officers were allowed in.

Once inside, they watched prostitute Sue Ann Morgan walk down the stairs and over to a bureau in the middle room of the first floor. There, Morgan took out a blue folder, made a notation and passed some cash over to Jones, who kept the money in a strongbox bolted to the bottom of a drawer. Morgan then went back upstairs to service a john. A second woman, Donna Marie Fisher, walked out of the kitchen and over to where the two officers were waiting. She asked them who was going first since the other prostitute was busy with another client. Petzar volunteered to go upstairs with Fisher to the third-floor bedroom.

What happened next was similar to the 1963 raid. Fisher asked Petzar what services he wanted. He made a selection and paid Fisher. She went downstairs to hand the money over to Jones before returning to the bedroom with a basin full of soapy water. Minutes later, Petzar revealed that he was a police officer and got dressed. He then escorted Fisher to the first floor.

On their way downstairs, Fisher opened the door to the second-floor bedroom where Morgan was busy having sex with a john. Fisher advised Morgan that they were "pinched." Naturally, that announcement brought an abrupt end to that particular transaction. Backup was called in, and the whorehouse was raided. The warrant was executed. Once again, police seized the marked money along with washbasins and trick books. Officers had to use tools to remove the strongbox from the drawer.

That July, Morgan and Fisher pled guilty to prostitution and were sentenced to fifteen days in jail with credit for time served. As for Jones, she was released after posting $500 bail. County court would have to deal with Jones one last time as a madam. Her whorehouse was raided on October 8, 1971, and Bessie was fined $500 and given a six-month suspended sentence for operating a bawdyhouse. From that point on, Jones was a victim of a string of crimes believed by some to have been perpetrated by the same interstate crime syndicate that supplied her with prostitutes.

On March 2, 1972, two men armed with a pistol forced their way into the whorehouse by pushing Jones away from the front door. Investigators released a description of the suspects and their vehicle, which resulted in the arrest of Edward Buti and Curtis Sawyer in McKeesport on charges of burglary, assault and attempted armed robbery. Two months later, on May 19, six men armed with a revolver barged into Bessie's Place and struck Jones across the head before tying and gagging her and three unidentified women. The men ransacked the house, taking money and jewelry.

A Cumberland County trial held that May resulted in a hung jury for Buti and Sawyer, and the prosecution decided later that fall not to retry the case.

Close-up of the tombstone of Bessie Jane Jones, whose murder in October 1972 remains a mystery. *Photo by Joseph David Cress.*

By that time, the primary witness and chief victim, Bessie Jane Jones, had been murdered in her whorehouse. Just before her death, the *Sentinel* reported how Jones was under investigation by the FBI, the state attorney general's office and the state police for her alleged connection to the syndicate.

Bessie Jones was found dead in her second-floor bedroom the morning of October 1, 1972. Sometime around 5:00 a.m., someone used a pair of nylons to tie her hands behind her back before stuffing a washcloth into her mouth. The murderer then took a knife and stabbed Jones three times in the left arm and torso. The fatal wound cut the pulmonary artery at the base of the heart, causing massive bleeding. Jones was laid to rest in the Andrews family plot in the Union Cemetery in Carlisle. She was so well known that newspapers in Philadelphia and Pittsburgh printed word of her death. On December 17, 1972, the *New York Sunday News* published a two-page picture story entitled "Good-bye Bessie."

The day of her murder, police stopped a taxicab on the Pennsylvania Turnpike about twelve miles west of Carlisle. Inside, police found Georgia Schneider with $2,789 stuffed inside her handbag and in her clothing. They arrested and charged her with murder and robbery. The prosecution's theory was that Schneider, a prostitute at the whorehouse, killed Jones as she was trying to steal money from the old madam. Schneider was defended by Herbert Goldstein (no relation to Hyman), who argued the murder showed signs of a professional hit conducted by the syndicate. The jury found Schneider not guilty.

Part IV

Devilish Doings

The wicked folk of Carlisle can take the term "all fired up" a bit too literally at times. The stories that follow all have the consequences of inflamed passions in common. We light the match with a tale of a local attorney seeking justice for a mysterious stranger whose actions helped to ignite the American Civil War. We add fuel with a story of a clever culprit whose efforts to get rid of a meddlesome bride took on explosive extremes. The flames burn bright with a rash of arson fires that sparked so much outrage, a town newspaper called for the death of any incendiary caught in the act. This sets the stage for the finale—a lethal love triangle that ended with the taking of innocent life and the death of a downtown icon.

Issue of Identity

The Extradition of Albert Hazlett

T he witness from Harpers Ferry had a difficult choice to make in identifying the fugitive. The two men in the Carlisle jail cell looked so much alike, it was hard to tell which one was Albert Hazlett, alias William Harrison. Mr. Copeland had to choose between the inmate who looked him squarely in the eye or the man who had just hung his head in shame. The witness chose false remorse over true defiance, pointing out the downcast prisoner and saying, "That is my man," but Sheriff Robert McCartney knew the truth. He was in on the ploy.

Sometime earlier, McCartney had warned defense attorney William Shearer that a new witness had arrived in town, claiming he could place Harrison among the men who launched a daring October 16, 1859 raid to seize arms from the federal arsenal at Harpers Ferry. Shearer had to think fast to fight this latest attempt at extradition. He asked the sheriff if he knew of anyone in Carlisle who looked like his client. McCartney confirmed there was such a fellow. Shearer then instructed the sheriff to ask that man to come down to the old jail at West High and North Bedford Streets.

Upon arrival, the volunteer was put into the same cell as the fugitive, and both men were asked to exchange clothes. While Harrison was instructed to stare directly at the witness, the imposter pretended to be ashamed, so when Copeland made his choice, McCartney was quick to point out the error. "Why that man was born and reared in Carlisle, and has never been out of the town," the sheriff said. For a while at least, the shell game worked, but this was not the first time the county official was sympathetic to the defense in this case. From the start, McCartney was a willing pawn in a game of legal chess, which ultimately resulted in Hazlett (alias Harrison) being executed as an enemy of Virginia for his role in the raid.

This strange collaboration began on October 22, 1859, shortly after Bill Houser and Charlie Campbell arrested a man who they believed was a fugitive from Harpers Ferry as the suspect was entering High Street on the west end of Carlisle. The *Carlisle American* reported there was slight resistance and that the stranger had four loaded revolvers, a Bowie knife, "some little money" and a circular advertising the book *The History of Slavery* in his possession. The stranger was described as being six feet tall and well built, with red hair and a thin, sandy beard. He was dressed in a red muslin shirt and dirty, dark pants. "He, as might be expected, is a rather hard looking individual, though under such circumstances every man is liable to be described as looking desperate and fit for any enterprise," the newspaper reported. The man claimed to be William Harrison of Indiana County, Pennsylvania. He was brought before the local district justice around noon but refused to answer any questions, proclaiming he was innocent.

Shearer was walking downtown just after twelve o'clock when he saw that a large crowd had gathered in front of the office of Squire Sponsler. Curious, he crossed the street and walked into the office, only to find Campbell, Houser and a tall, rawboned man sitting in some chairs. When he asked what was going on, Houser told Shearer the stranger was Captain John Cook, a prominent leader among John Brown's men. He had been tracked down and apprehended after escaping from Chambersburg. Sponsler was in the process of writing up the paperwork to grant Houser and Campbell the authority to transport their prisoner to Virginia to face trial.

However, Shearer could not believe the stranger was Cook, whom the newspapers described as being an effeminate-looking man with long, light hair and blue eyes. But Houser did not care who the suspect was, just that he was one of the raiders. On realizing that Shearer was an attorney, Harrison asked, "Will you see that I have justice done me?" Shearer agreed to represent the man and warned Sponsler he had no right to draw up papers sending Harrison, a Pennsylvania resident, to a different state without court approval. This was later confirmed by Sponsler's attorney, William Penrose.

None of this mattered to Houser, who insisted on taking the fugitive to Virginia. Just as he and Campbell were preparing to depart with Harrison, Shearer threatened to press kidnapping charges against them. Expecting trouble, Shearer asked the sheriff and a deputy to stand just outside the office door and arrest Houser and Campbell if necessary. The two men relented, and the stranger was temporarily spared from extradition, but Sponsler exercised his right to jail the man. Shearer, along with other attorneys for the defense, filed a writ of habeas corpus on behalf of Harrison in the county court. This prompted a series of extradition hearings before Judge James H. Graham, with Judge Frederick Watts of Cumberland County serving as counsel for Virginia.

During the first hearing, held on October 26, Watts presented a warrant from Pennsylvania governor William Packer requesting the release of Albert Hazlett to Virginia authorities. Watts proved that revolvers found on the stranger were of similar manufacture as those used by the insurgents during the raid and that the appearance of the suspect closely matched the description of Hazlett as given by witnesses at the scene. However, since there were no witnesses called who could verify that the man in custody was the fugitive Hazlett, Graham remanded the prisoner back to county jail and set Saturday, October 29, as a follow-up hearing for prosecutors to present witnesses from Harpers Ferry.

In his writings on the case, Shearer documented two different occasions where he enlisted the help of McCartney to call into question the ability of

This circa 1875 photograph shows a view of South Hanover Street taken from the square. The Carlisle Market House is on the left, and the old county courthouse is on the right.

prosecution witnesses to identify his client during the visits they had made to the county jail. Shearer made no mention of the precise dates when each incident happened, but the visits probably happened before the October 29 hearing. The *Carlisle Herald* reported the same witnesses who swore to the identity of the prisoner in the courtroom failed to recognize him earlier from visiting the jail.

On the first occasion, Shearer had received word from McCartney that two or three men were in Carlisle to take his client to Virginia. When asked, the sheriff explained that the men were still at their hotel smoking their after-breakfast cigars before heading over to the jail. Shearer advised McCartney that he was in charge of keeping prisoners, not pointing them out to authorities. "If they want him, they ought to know him," he told the sheriff. "Let them pick him out."

Shearer then asked McCartney to set all one hundred inmates at the county jail loose inside the main corridor. When the travelers arrived, they asked the sheriff which prisoner was Hazlett, but McCartney told them that he had been warned by Shearer not to spot the prisoner for them. "You ought to know the man," the sheriff said. "Look in there, he is there." Sure enough, the men could not pick Hazlett out from the crowd of prisoners. A short time later, a second party came up from Virginia claiming they could identify Hazlett. Again, McCartney warned Shearer. This led to the ploy of the downcast imposter.

On February 22, 1860, the *Carlisle American* ran a story on what Hazlett told a Charles Town court after being sentenced to death by hanging. In his statement, the recently tried and convicted man continued to proclaim his innocence and challenged the witness testimony of October 29, 1859.

> *I am innocent of the charge in which I have been convicted. I deny ever having committed murder or ever having to contemplate murder, or ever having associated with anyone having such an intention. Some of the witnesses have sworn to things…which are positively false…Again, Mr. Copeland testified that I was sitting on a stool when he entered the cell at Carlisle; this I deny. I was sitting on a blanket back against the wall, and another man was on the stool. Copeland also said there were only two men in the cell; this is false, as there were four other white men with me.*

Although Copeland misidentified the fugitive in jail, he swore under oath the prisoner was one of the raiders. During the hearing, Copeland testified that, while he saw a flash come from the prisoner's rifle, he could not tell whether it was aimed at anyone. A man was shot in the street at about the same time. Another witness, by the name of Colliss, told the court he and a neighbor talked with the prisoner in the street and examined his rifle to see how it was loaded. At first, they thought the stranger was a militiaman on his way to the Winchester Fair, but then two similarly armed men came up, seized them as prisoners and marched them to the armory where they were detained.

There were, however, discrepancies among the witnesses as to the appearance of Hazlett. One said he had whiskers that came to a point at the chin but no mustache, while another said he had a light beard and a light mustache. One witness saw Hazlett wearing a red flannel jacket with side pockets, while another said he wore a striped shirt. Despite this, Watts argued it was clear that the prisoner had been present and participated in the raid. He reminded the court the revolvers found on the stranger matched those found on the insurgents.

This photograph of Albert Hazlett (alias William Harrison) is from the Boyd B. Stutler Collection. *Courtesy of the West Virginia State Archives.*

Shearer argued that the proof of identity was insufficient and therefore did not warrant the judge delivering the prisoner into the custody of Virginia authorities. The defense claimed there was no evidence the man in custody was Albert Hazlett, the name specifically mentioned in the requisition from Virginia. They asked Graham to discharge the prisoner or at least commit him to the custody of the sheriff until further proof of his identity could be obtained. The judge agreed with both sides, saying that while the prosecution proved that the man in custody participated in the raid, the defense was correct in concluding insufficient evidence existed that the prisoner was indeed Hazlett. The judge called for a third hearing to be held on November 5.

While the stranger calling himself Harrison denied any involvement in the raid, history records that Hazlett was assigned to guard the arsenal building with Osborne Perry Anderson, a free black recruited by Brown in Canada. A Pennsylvania native, Hazlett first met Brown in Kansas in 1858, where they fought as "Free State" guerrillas against pro-slavery settlers trying to control the political destiny of that disputed territory.

On the afternoon of October 17, 1859, Hazlett and Anderson heard a commotion outside the arsenal building and realized there was nothing they could do to help Brown and the other raiders, so they decided to escape amid the confusion. In his book, *A Voice from Harpers Ferry*, Anderson described how he and Hazlett paddled across the Potomac River in a stolen boat before escaping to the Kennedy Farm, the main staging area for the raid.

The two men then fled north into Pennsylvania where they separated. Anderson continued into Canada while Hazlett turned northeast toward Chambersburg, a transit point for weapons used in the raid. This led to reports that John Cook was lurking near Chambersburg when it was really Hazlett visiting the home where Mrs. Cook was a boarder. When civilians surrounded the house, Hazlett fled, pursued by Houser and Campbell.

Shearer visited his mysterious client the night of November 4. During that conversation, the man said he was with John Brown in Kansas. As Shearer left, the stranger asked for a plug of tobacco. The attorney passed on this request to the sheriff and, in doing so, cost his client his life as McCartney went back and examined the man's cell and found part of the wall concealed by a blanket missing. It was later determined that Mark Scott, an African American barber, was dispatched to Carlisle by a follower of John Brown with a horse and buggy, a rope ladder and instructions to help the prisoner escape. This plan was foiled when the sheriff put Hazlett in a different cell.

In his writings, Shearer believed the request for tobacco had been interpreted by McCartney as a warning not to allow the prisoner to escape. This prompted him to check the cell and transfer the prisoner. The next morning, November 5, McCartney told Shearer, "That client of yours is the most stupid man I ever saw in my life. You know when I was sent down with him, it was very dark, as dark as midnight…and if he had just given me a little push I would have fallen over into the gutter." This statement confirmed for Shearer that McCartney knew Hazlett wanted to escape and that the sheriff wanted to let him go but had misinterpreted the request for tobacco.

That same morning, defense attorneys asked the court for a continuance. They were waiting for a response from a letter sent from the State of Indiana to witnesses who could testify in support of the prisoner's alibi that he was not in Harpers Ferry at the time of the raid. Watts opposed this request, saying the defense had two weeks to produce evidence to back the alibi. Besides, there was nothing in the letter to suggest the two witnesses had

This 1955 photograph by James Steinmetz shows the courtroom of the old county courthouse on the square.

evidence contrary to what was already presented in court. Watts now had a warrant with the name "William Harrison."

In a written decision, Judge Graham ordered the prisoner released into the custody of Virginia. He explained that it was the prisoner who first identified himself as Harrison and had a writ of habeas corpus granted under that name. Further, the judge ruled the prisoners knew where he was on October 16–18 and yet offered no statement as to his whereabouts. "We are not called to pass on the guilt of the prisoner," Graham wrote. "The only question before us is the issue of identity." Hazlett was led away.

A sympathetic crowd followed the prisoner from the jail to the afternoon train bound for the South. The *Carlisle American* reported how tears were shed for the alleged fugitive amid charges of injustice against the court for not granting the continuance. The newspapers urged protestors to carefully review Graham's decision: "We feel confident [it] will convince any right-thinking persons that justice had been done to the State of Virginia while the prisoner had been given all the latitude permitted by the fair and impartial laws of Pennsylvania."

Shearer not only arranged for Hazlett to have legal counsel in Charles Town but also furnished the defense team with an important piece of evidence. Shearer said that the Sharps rifle the prisoner had when he was arrested had never been fired. He explained how these rifles were so neatly polished at the factory that powder residue from any discharge would have so discolored the finish that the manufacturer would have had to remove the blemish.

Defense attorneys in Virginia wrote Shearer, stating that, at one point, they were confident of either an acquittal or a hung jury. However, the verdict was guilty after jurors were hounded throughout the night by a crowd yelling, "Hang him or we will hang you!" On February 16, 1860, the *American Volunteer* had this to say about the conviction of Hazlett:

> *Poor fellow, we really feel sympathy for this young man, for he was evidentially led into wickedness and crime by the advice of older heads. His appearance is that of a mild man, but appearances are often deceptive. The fact that he took deliberate aim at and fired upon citizens of Harpers Ferry…Citizens who have never harmed him was evidence he was willing to obey to the letter the orders of his desperate and bloodthirsty chief, old Brown.*

Hazlett was executed at 12:08 p.m. on March 22, 1860, on gallows erected on the exact same spot Brown and other raiders were put to death. Prior to that, the fugitive wrote Shearer a thank-you letter stating that he had been more than a brother to him. He signed the letter, "Your friend through endless eternity…William L. Harrison."

Infernal Machine

The Story of Charley Foulk

T he front door fell with a mighty crash upon the vestibule floor. Someone had forced it violently from its hinges in their haste to unleash hell with an infernal machine. Former sheriff Robert McCartney was asleep inside the stone house at 123 South Bedford Street the morning of January 26, 1876. The intruders barged in around 1:00 a.m., rousing the old man from slumber, but this rude awakening was about to turn potentially lethal.

Five minutes later, the bomb exploded with such horrific force that local journalists compared the blast to an earthquake in the way it shook the ground. The noise was described as an artillery barrage or a sudden clap of thunder. The *Carlisle Mirror* reported how the detonation lit the atmosphere like the "flash of the most vivid lightning." In an instant, all window frames and shutters in the façade were blown out and reduced to piles of splintered wood and pulverized glass.

The explosion had so much force that cellar doors in adjoining homes were blown from their hinges and a large curb stone in front of the target building was hurled across the street and through a sturdy fence. Windowpanes were shattered in every house on the block and at the German Lutheran Church, which stood on the northwest corner of South Bedford and East Pomfret Streets.

The roar of the bomb destroyed the early morning calm as it echoed through town and into the countryside, where it woke an employee of Kast's Tannery, which was located about five miles outside Carlisle. Figuring a vat had just exploded, the worker roused his boss only to be proven wrong. There were other sounds of panic. "The piercing shriek of

This circa 1870 photograph by A.A. Line shows the Old German Lutheran Church on the northwest corner of South Bedford and East Pomfret Streets. The stone house that was allegedly bombed twice by Charley Foulk was located about a half block to the south on the east side of Bedford Street. A day-care center sits there now.

a female rent the air which betoken something horrible had happened," the *American Volunteer* reported.

The shriek probably belonged to Maria Stringfellow, who lived in the stone house with McCartney. Journalists at that time could not confirm whether the dwelling was owned by her or the former sheriff. There was speculation that she was his housekeeper or that he was her boarder.

Questions about their relationship led to gossip and scandal. What is known is that Maria also went by the last name Foulk and had claimed to her dying day to be married to a Civil War veteran named Charley Foulk, who was widely regarded as the black sheep of an otherwise respected Carlisle family. Her persistence in this claim may be the reason why the stone house was bombed not once but twice within two months, with Charley emerging as the prime suspect each time.

Local historian D.W. Thompson wrote a book on the life and times of Charley. In it, he traced the origin of Maria's marriage claim to a party both had attended sometime between 1862 and 1870. During the party, guests noticed how Charley and Maria had romantic feelings for one another, so someone suggested they go through a wedding ceremony together. A local official was present who knew the ritual. Only later did Charley tell Maria he had not intended marriage. He thought everyone present had taken the mock wedding as a parlor game, but Maria was convinced they were married. Given what happened later, Thompson believed the official present may have been Sheriff McCartney and that somehow the old man was an interloper in the affair, making him and Maria a target of vengeance.

Surprisingly, no one was hurt in the first bombing. "With windows and doors crashing about them and bits of flaming cloth and paper sailing through the rooms, the occupants…escaped all injury save fright," the *Sentinel* reported. The building, with its thick stone walls, withstood the shock, but burning fragments of rope dotted the carpet in most every room, causing a headache for firefighters responding to the incident. The outcome could have been far worse.

Evidence at the scene suggested the real intention of the bombers was to break open the door and throw the device, dubbed the "infernal machine" by the press, deeper into the entry where it could do more damage. But fate intervened, and the explosion took place right in front of the door.

There was debate at first over whether the explosive used was dynamite, nitroglycerin or a combination with a cotton cloth encased in a coil of rope, which was then wrapped in paper and copper wire. Particles resembling burnt fuse were picked up at or near the scene. The *Carlisle Mirror* reported that the device, upon exploding, broke into two parts—one of which was recovered by McCartney. Based on its dimensions, the newspaper estimated the original bomb was about sixteen inches long and three to four inches in diameter.

News of the bombing spread rapidly through Carlisle, and by morning, the first of hundreds of visitors braved a drenching rain to visit the crime scene. Word of the attack was flashed across the wire service to outlets nationwide, and the local press responded with its own brand of outrage. "We have in our midst wretches so inhuman…as to attempt not only the destruction of property, but the lives of our people," the *Sentinel* reported. The *American Volunteer* saw the incident as both a badge of shame and a call to action:

> *We bow our heads submissively as we ponder over the fact our town is disgraced with fiends who dare, in the still hour of midnight, to jeopardize the lives of a whole neighborhood and innocent people by an explosion of an infernal machine. There was no doubt that murder most foul was intended.*
>
> *A feeling of dread has pervaded our entire community. No one knows what other midnight horror is in store for us. Eternal vigilance should be the watch word. The lives and property of our citizens…must be better protected in the future. This can best be done by putting on duty an efficient police force. Until this is done, we are not safe from midnight robbers, incendiaries and dynamite agents.*

As authorities investigated, conflicting stories emerged over what had happened that morning. Some witnesses claimed they heard the hasty footsteps of men moving rapidly up Chapel Alley near the target house. Others saw a carriage being driven away at full speed down Bedford Street at the same time as the explosion. "Many rumors were floated in regards to this damnable affair," the *Volunteer* reported.

Ultimately, Charley Foulk and Jacques Noble were arrested and put on trial that April in connection with the first bombing. While McCartney and Stringfellow testified to seeing the defendants near the house soon after the blast, "Foulk proved by the testimony of a dozen or more respectable witnesses that he was in Harrisburg at the time," the *Volunteer* reported. The newspaper went on to add, "Noble…proved an alibi with such unerring certainty and by such respectable witnesses that no doubt was left on the minds of the jury…of his innocence. Altogether, public sympathy has been drawn to the side of the defendants in this case." The *Carlisle Herald* reported how the jury was out for only fifteen minutes before returning with a verdict of not guilty for both men.

This sort of outcome was typical for Foulk, who had a knack for dodging justice for alleged criminal deeds. Many in Carlisle regarded him as a folk hero or clever playboy. A gambler, Foulk never wanted for money, and his ties to an influential family tree may have been his saving grace when he faced charges such as murder, assault with intent to kill, arson and inciting a riot.

Stephen Foulk, a son of a Welsh immigrant, founded the local family as an early settler of the headwaters of the Letort Spring Run. A stonemason and building contractor, he built the First Presbyterian Church, the oldest public building in Carlisle, in the city's square. His son, Dr. George Foulk, practiced medicine in town all his life and was the father of two sons who were also physicians.

Willis Foulk, father of Charley, served as county prothonotary and was believed to have been an officer in the Pennsylvania militia during the War of 1812. Charley was born in 1837 and was about ten years old when Willis died. Charley would later serve with the Pennsylvania volunteers during the Civil War before marrying Sarah Lytle in 1870. She was the daughter of one of the town's chief constables.

Charley's first brush with the law took place in early 1863, when he was arrested as an accomplice to murder in the March 17 shooting of Corporal John Barney, a soldier stationed at Carlisle Barracks. Barney was in charge of a detachment sent out to find two soldiers who were absent without leave from the post. During their patrol, Barney was shot and mortally wounded while investigating a brawl between two women at the corner of North East Street and Locust Avenue.

After the prosecution rested its case during the murder trial, defense attorney William H. Miller asked the court to instruct the jury to find Charley not guilty. Miller argued none of the testimony directly linked his client to the shooting. Judge James Graham agreed, and the jury acquitted Charley without even leaving the box. Miller then called the former defendant as his first witness.

But before he would testify, Charley insisted on asking Graham whether he could ever be tried again for killing Barney. After being reassured that double jeopardy applies, Charley surprised everyone in the courtroom by confessing to the murder, claiming he had killed Barney only in self-defense after the soldier attacked him.

Three years later, in August 1866, Charley Foulk and Henry Dixon were put on trial for arson, charged with burning the Emory Methodist Episcopal Chapel. The chief prosecution witness was an accomplice named Charles Harkness, who told jurors he was with both men when they fired the building. Defense attorneys responded with a sworn statement by Harkness, which contradicted part of his testimony. This, along with strong evidence in support of an alibi, resulted in a verdict of not guilty.

In January 1867, Foulk and Dixon were again put on trial, this time charged with setting fire to a stable belonging to Abner Bentz of Carlisle.

While this trial resulted in a conviction, the judge decided to set aside the verdict, citing dissatisfaction with the nature of the evidence. A motion for a new trial was accepted. In April 1867, the district attorney reviewed this case and realized there was no new evidence that could better prove the arson charge. He chose not to prosecute, and once again, Charley Foulk escaped punishment by the courts.

Between the arson trials, an incident took place on December 10, 1866, involving the former sheriff. As the story goes, McCartney was walking down South Bedford Street around 9:30 p.m. when he passed a man wearing a soldier's overcoat and a fur cap. Suddenly, the man turned and fired a load of buckshot at McCartney. One shot passed through the sheriff's coat sleeve, but the majority of the load struck a nearby fence. McCartney was not hurt, and the man escaped.

The assailant was later identified as Charley Foulk, who was arrested on a charge of assault with intent to kill. When the district attorney reviewed this case in April 1867, he determined that not enough evidence existed to convict Charley, so an offer was made to drop the charge in exchange for Foulk posting a $5,000 bond to keep the peace. So while the prosecution could not prove its case, it appears that Charley was not convinced he

This circa 1890 photograph by A.A. Line shows the view looking down South Bedford Street from East High Street.

could prove his innocence. Why else would he accept the terms and pay the modern-day equivalent of $77,000?

Less than nine years later, on January 26, 1876, the first of two explosions rocked the house that once stood at 123 South Bedford Street. Charley Foulk was free on bail and awaiting trial for the first bombing when a second explosion took place at around 9:00 p.m. on March 28, 1876. Newspapers described it as a dark and rainy night. The structural damage was more extensive because the bomber had taken the time to contain the blast by placing the device on the vestibule floor before closing the front door. The shock wave was felt all over town, and the explosion was heard as far away as two miles. The *Carlisle Mirror* described the aftermath:

> *Occupants in adjoining houses for a square on each side…were startled beyond description. Hundreds of people were on the spot, gazing bewilderingly upon the ruin before them. The front door, shutters and window sash were broken into and across the street. The door frame torn and shattered…The walls surrounding it cracked and broken.*
>
> *Inside everything was a ruin…Partition walls were completely demolished. The floors and ceiling ripped up and broken in holes large enough for a man to drop through…Ornaments and portable articles were smashed into unrecognizable pieces…The walls having been spread to such an extent as to cause the roof to drop in.*

Again, no one inside was injured, but there were many close calls. McCartney had been downstairs only minutes before the blast to get a pitcher of water. He was in the upstairs bedroom taking prescription medicine when the explosion threw him against a wall and blew the medicine right out of his hand. Meanwhile, in the same room, Maria Stringfellow (alias Foulk) was lying in bed resting when the blast tore out a huge hole in the floor only a few feet away. In its coverage, the *Sentinel* identified Maria as the property owner.

Her nephew was sleeping in an adjacent room when the device exploded. The force of the blast was so powerful that it threw him to the floor and reduced the headboard of his bed to splinters. No one outside was injured, but a negro barber named Green was lifted ten feet into the air by the explosion as he was walking past the home. The umbrella Green was carrying sailed away into the night and was still missing two days later. The *Mirror* painted a grim picture with words:

It is universally believed that the perpetrators of these crimes will not desist until their ends are accomplished, no matter what the consequences are and what injuries are inflicted upon those who live in the vicinity. So strong is this conviction that the parties that have rented the neighboring houses for the next year have thrown up their leases, preferring the risk of having no place to move to rather than live in the fated locality.

In April 1876, Charley Foulk and Jacques Noble were tried in county court on charges related to the first bombing. As aforementioned, testimony by McCartney and Stringfellow was overwhelmed by an effective alibi from the defense. After reports of the second bombing showed that McCartney was still living with Stringfellow, public sympathy shifted in Charley's favor, who after all had proved his innocence in court and was looked upon as a victim of persecution. All this scandal damaged the credibility and social standing of the bomb victims.

It is said that one night, Charley added insult to injury by gathering five of his friends into a carriage, which was then driven up and down Bedford Street past the bomb-shattered home. The six men mocked McCartney and Stringfellow by singing the popular old hymn "Hold the Fort" over and over again at the top of their lungs. As a result, McCartney pressed charges of inciting a riot, leading to the arrest of Charley along with his friends John Low, Ed Lytle, Tom Wilsted, Harry Grove and Jacques Noble. They were all put on trial in August 1876. Figuring everyone has a right to sing in public, the jury failed to see how the incident was a riot, and all six men were acquitted of the charge.

No arrests were ever made in connection with the second bombing. Thompson wrote how public opinion against the bomb victims prompted the district attorney to charge McCartney and Stringfellow with perjury for allegedly bearing false witness against Charley Foulk. The basis for the perjury charge was never argued in open court. Despite this, McCartney was put on trial for perjury but offered no defense. He was ordered to spend ninety days in county jail and pay about fifty dollars in fines and costs. The former sheriff served out his sentence in the very same jail where he housed Albert Hazlett seventeen years before. Meanwhile, the perjury case against Maria was postponed until January 1877, when a local judge dismissed it because it was causing nothing but scandal.

But justice was about to catch up to Charley. For years, an arson ring operated in Carlisle, burning down stables and other structures across town. The large volume of fires in 1876 prompted town council to secretly hire an undercover investigator to expose the ring. In April 1877, authorities arrested William and Jacques Noble for the arson of the John Noble property the previous October. Upon his arrest, William Noble turned informant against Charley, and in August 1877, the court indicted Foulk on arson and other related charges.

By that time, Charley had left town for the western frontier but was arrested in late May 1878 and transported back to Carlisle in mid-June. When the train pulled into town in front of the old county jail, two hundred men, women and children were there to catch a glimpse of the elusive criminal. Bail was fixed at $2,750, and bonds were posted for his release. Charley promptly left Carlisle a second time and settled in Hot Springs, Arkansas, where he adopted the alias of Charles Watson and became part owner of a gambling house and saloon called the Owl. There, Charley became embroiled in a power struggle between two factions fighting for control of the town. Ultimately, this led to a shooting war, during which Charley was involved in a gunfight with a local newspaper editor whose sympathies favored the opposing faction. On November 30, 1884, Charley Foulk was shot and killed while riding in a buggy down the main street of town. There was speculation his death could have been revenge for the ambush and assassination of rival gang members earlier in the war; there was also evidence that it may have been an accidental shooting by a police officer named Carter Brutus. Carlisle residents were notified of Charley's death on December 5, 1884. Colonel William Foulk of Pittsburgh arranged to have his younger brother's remains shipped back to their hometown of Carlisle.

Charley Foulk was put on public display prior to burial. "Viewing the body satisfied a number of doubters who had said all along that Foulk was too smart to be shot by any policeman," Thompson wrote in his book. It also put to rest rumors that the coffin was empty or held some other corpse.

The arrival of the corpse triggered speculation that Maria would reassert her belief that she was Charley's wife. A large crowd had gathered at the train station to see if she would claim the body, but Maria did not appear. However, she did hire a man to drive her in a carriage that traveled alongside the hearse the whole way to the Old Graveyard on East South Street. There, Maria Stringfellow stood by quietly as a local pastor said some final words before the remains were lowered into the ground.

"To Foulk's already unusual record, we now add the fact that he was the only man in local history to be mourned at his funeral by two rival widows," Thompson wrote. On Maria, he added, "We do not know what her private thoughts were. She might have well felt as much triumph as sorrow. Twenty

Burial site of Charley Foulk in the Old Graveyard on East South Street in Carlisle. *Photo by Joseph David Cress.*

years before, she had wanted to marry Foulk and had insisted all her life that she had done so. For this unwelcome devotion, Foulk twice wrecked her house and nearly killed her."

The *Sentinel* newspaper had this to say in retrospect:

> *The violent death of Charles H. Foulk contains a lesson and a warning to many young men…who seem by their actions to be emulating his career. It is certain as the laws of the tides that a man who defies society and scorns its laws will, in the end, become a criminal…despised by every man, or a fugitive from justice…unless he should die a murderer's death on the scaffold. Society draws a breath of relief when such men die.*
>
> *But there is another lesson in Foulk's life that our church-going reformers may well study. In some things, he was as tender-hearted as a woman. Daring and fearless as he was, many a strong man has seen his lip quiver and his eye moisten at the mention of his mother's name. There was a bright lining of the dark cloud of his wasted life and if the right influence at the right time had been brought to bear, who knows but a changed, reformed and better life might have been the result.*

Fire Fiends

An Arson Ring Broken

The town clock struck two on that soggy morning just as John DeHuff was climbing down the fence. A dog was heard barking from a house above the tannery, which, despite the steady drizzle, was about to be engulfed in flame. If one believes Henry Grove, a codefendant in the arson case, it had been an eventful night for DeHuff, a volunteer firefighter who had lost his first slow match or fireball when he fell into the Letort Spring Run the first time he tried to trespass onto the tannery property the morning of Sunday, November 19, 1876.

On the witness stand, Grove testified how it was DeHuff who suggested the conspirators try out the fire engine he had just repaired. The friends were sitting around the Cumberland firehouse drinking whiskey after a Saturday night on the town. After taking another swig, DeHuff, Grove and Jacob Widner talked about committing arson. Widner wanted to start a fire at the tannery near the creek on the south end of East Street, but Grove would later testify to saying, "We had better not, we may get caught." DeHuff then gathered up some waste rags and saturated the cloth in coal oil before rolling it up into a bundle to create his first slow match of the evening. The men then left the firehouse.

"We went down Bedford Street to South Street and then down South to East," Grove told jurors during his January 1877 trial. "I stood on the corner to watch as Widner and DeHuff went around the tannery towards the spring." Moments later, DeHuff crossed the street to where Grove was standing. He was soaked to the skin but still determined to fire the tannery. "We returned to the engine house where DeHuff assembled

This 1889 photograph by A.A. Line shows the old Cumberland Fire Company building on South Bedford Street. The fire apparatus is on the street in preparation for the Firemen's Convention parade. The apparatus on the right is Cumberland's George B. McClellan steamer with the hero's portrait on the smokestack.

another ball and said 'Damn, if I don't make a good one this time,'" Grove testified. Grove then led the way as the men returned to the scene where he saw Widner and DeHuff scale the fence near the bark mill where the second bundle of oil-soaked rags was placed. But just like the first time, DeHuff was stymied by a mishap. He had struck all his wooden matches but could not get the bundle to ignite. Finally, he had to ask Widner for some more matches.

Eventually, DeHuff lit the fire before climbing back over the fence at about 2:00 a.m. The three men then went up East Street to Pomfret Street, where DeHuff parted company to head home to change his clothes and to be there when the fire alarm went off. Grove and Widner walked down Bedford Street to South Street and stood on the northwest corner to watch the tannery burn. At first, the flames had died down, and Widner suggested they return to the scene to stoke the fire, but Grove convinced them not to do it. Instead, the two men took another drink from the whiskey bottle, and Widner ridiculed the Carlisle police by pointing out arsonists had just set fire to a building right under the nose of Constable Hays, who lived on East Street.

If only they knew that an undercover detective on the secret payroll of borough council had already infiltrated the ranks of the "firebugs" and was getting ready to turn them in. On that night, as the conspirators looked on, Grove noticed how the fire flared up suddenly. He said to Widner, "We must get out of this." A short time later, Grove met up again with DeHuff at the tannery fire where they both used the recently repaired engine to fight a fire they both helped to set.

The first alarm was at about 2:30 a.m. The response was quick, but the flames had spread so rapidly that the entire rear section of the wood-frame building was virtually consumed before the volunteers could lay out hose lines to spray water on the fire. Not surprisingly, the Cumberland Fire Company was the first on the scene, courtesy of Grove, who raised the alarm early. Even so, the *Carlisle Mirror* reported that all effort to put out the fire was futile, and "in an incredibly short space of time, the entire establishment was a sea of flame." Most everything was destroyed, including much of the machinery and about eighty cords of bark kept in a shed near where the fire was set. There was speculation that, out of the six hundred or so hides, a small portion could be saved. The building was owned by Calvin Clendenin and leased by Frank Hopkins, both of whom had some insurance.

A strong east wind was blowing through that part of Carlisle, but wet roofs from the morning drizzle prevented the spread of the arson fire. While a comfort to some, the soggy weather was a reminder to others of just how brazen the firebugs had become. This was described in a November 21, 1876 article published in the *Carlisle Mirror*: "Ordinarily wet nights have given people the assurance of safety from fire while they slumber, but the fiends have so often of late applied their destructive torch to properties within this borough, determined to rob us of even that little solace from bad weather by selecting such nights for their scoundralism."

Yet arson was one of the most popular crimes in Carlisle in the mid- to late nineteenth century. The year 1876 was an especially bad one for fires set by "incendiaries"—a common newspaper term for arsonists. Conditions at the time were conducive for a firebug infestation. Many businesses and large homes had their own stables—a popular target since most were wooden outbuildings located at the rear of the properties and filled with hay and straw. There were rumors that an arson ring made up of thrill

This circa 1865 photograph by John Choate shows volunteers with the Good Will Hose Company in front of the Shearer building at 24 West High Street. It depicts an example of how fires were fought using late nineteenth-century methods and apparatus.

seekers and first responders was operating in Carlisle, and that the fires were set purely for the excitement of racing to the scene and competing with rival fire companies. Neither the public nor the press was amused. In an editorial published on November 2, 1876, the *Carlisle Herald* summed up the frustrations of local residents:

We are not alarmists, but the present state of affairs is perfectly appalling; there is no protection to either life or property. Is it not high time that town council take some active measures towards ferreting out these ruthless villains who infest this community and bring them to justice? Does fear deter them from taking the proper steps? Or are we to fold our arms and permit these wretches to reduce the town to ashes?

The newspaper did not know that the borough council had, in late October, secretly agreed to pay John Morrison ten dollars a week to go undercover. Operating out of his home on North Street, Morrison would frequent local saloons, posing as an arsonist to gain the trust of those the local press had dubbed firebugs or "fire fiends." Information led him to suspect that members of the Cumberland Fire Company were involved in the arson ring. Sources told Morrison the conspirators met on certain evenings at the engine house located on the southwest corner of Liberty Alley and Bedford Street. There they would play cards while discussing future targets.

One night, Morrison went to the meeting place early and hid in the ash pit sunk below floor level and beneath the steam pumper, the George B. McClellan. He passed his findings on to the authorities, who not only arrested Grove, DeHuff and Widner for the tannery fire but also William Hendel and Charles O'Donnell for their role in other arson fires. In January 1877, Grove pled guilty to setting fire to the Noaker family stable. Together, Grove and Morrison became the key prosecution witnesses in trials held that month.

Morrison testified he saw Grove, Widner and DeHuff the night of the tannery fire in the saloon Hendel operated in the basement of the Bixler building at Market House Alley and High Street. The detective left the bar with the trio at about 11:45 p.m. on Saturday, November 18, 1876. As they were parting ways, Morrison overheard Widner tell the others he would like to "make a racket on the tannery tonight." Morrison went home to bed.

Two weeks later, Morrison was talking with Grove, who recalled how slow matches were made at the engine house before the conspirators walked over to the tannery. Grove told Morrison that when DeHuff and Widner decided to run home, it fell to him to light the fireball and then return to the engine house to sound the alarm. Grove denied this version on the witness stand.

The detective also testified to having a conversation with DeHuff shortly after Grove was arrested. Morrison claimed that DeHuff suggested setting fire to a stable to draw suspicion away from Grove, who was in police custody. Maintaining his cover, Morrison suggested that DeHuff

This circa 1890 photograph shows Harry Gibb driving the steam fire engine John Lindner by a team of horses from the Cumberland Fire Company station on East Louther Street.

instead set fire to a different stable—one that he knew was under police surveillance. No fire took place.

The defense called Mr. and Mrs. Abram DeHuff, who testified their son returned home and went right upstairs to bed between midnight and 12:30 a.m. the morning of November 19. The parents claimed that John was still sleeping when the fire alarm was sounded just after 2:00 a.m. This alibi was reinforced by neighbor T.F. Reighter, who testified he saw a sober John DeHuff pull on his clothing as he left the family home on North East Street to respond to the fire call.

Taking the stand in his own defense, John DeHuff explained how he had left the engine house for home shortly after telling Grove and Widner that he wanted nothing to do with setting fire to the tannery. DeHuff testified he was not at the tannery that morning and only learned of the fire after a next-door neighbor knocked on the partition wall to wake him up shortly after the alarm. The jury took just two hours to convict DeHuff, Grove and Widner of arson in the tannery fire.

During his second trial, held in January 1877, John DeHuff had a more colorful alibi to a charge of attempted arson filed against him for the Greenfield stable fire of June 16, 1875. The stable was located on the south side of Liberty Alley, about 150 feet behind the market house that once stood on the town square. The Market House space is now occupied by the new Cumberland County Courthouse. In 1875, the stable was owned by L.T. Greenfield, who later played a part in hiring Morrison as a detective.

DeHuff told jurors he and O'Donnell were drinking beer with some women at the house of Mrs. Givler until about midnight the morning of the fire. On their way home, the two men walked past William Goodyear, who was sleeping in the grass along Liberty Alley about fifty feet from the bakery that he owned. DeHuff and O'Donnell testified under oath that they only learned of the stable fire the day after it happened. During cross-examination, DeHuff told jurors he was unaware that the Givler home was a house of ill repute and that he had no knowledge of the marital status of the three women who lived there. "I never stayed there all night," he said.

DeHuff denied claims made by Goodyear that codefendants shook him awake to tell him about the fire at the stable. "There was no such conversation," DeHuff said. Goodyear testified the two men not only woke him from a drunken stupor around 2:00 a.m. but also walked down the alley with him to the bakery where they parted company shortly after constable George Wetzel showed up.

Wetzel testified he was near the bakery when he heard people talking and went over to investigate. Upon arrival, he caught a glimpse of DeHuff and O'Donnell just as they were pulling their collars up and their hats down before walking away. Taylor Morrison testified he was walking down the alley at about 2:00 a.m. when he saw Goodyear sleeping on the grass and DeHuff and O'Donnell walking rapidly down the side of the alley.

Another witness, Charles Taylor, testified he was on his way to the Market House shortly after 2:00 a.m., when he encountered DeHuff and O'Donnell near the Cumberland engine house. Both men were walking at a moderate pace away from Liberty Alley and toward Bedford Street. This witness continued on his way until he heard the sound of a door being forced open and noticed the stable was on fire. He helped to extinguish the flames that were blazing upward in one corner, about three or four feet high. It was William Noble who spotted the fire as a strange light coming from the stable. After dropping off his tools at the Market House, Noble raced back to the scene and, with help from Charles Taylor and Moses

Watson, tore the door off its hinges and threw planks on the fire to smother it until they could get water.

The jury found DeHuff and O'Donnell guilty of attempted arson. The third and final trial involved Hendel, who was charged with setting fire to Rheem's Hall, which was located behind the old courthouse on the square. The fire was put out in time. Once the largest public building in Carlisle, Rheem's Hall housed both an opera house and the *Sentinel* newspaper office.

This detail of an 1872 map of Carlisle was copied from the *Atlas of Cumberland County, Pennsylvania*. It depicts the section of town impacted by the arson ring.

Grove testified that, on the evening of December 8, 1876, he had a conversation with Hendel in his saloon, during which the firebug complained about the technique others in the arson ring used to fire the tannery. He then explained to Grove that the best way to manufacture a slow match or fireball was to first take a twelve-foot cotton wick and double it six times. The wick was then soaked in a solution of gunpowder, dried and then attached to one-quarter pound of powder at one end and a safety fuse at the other end.

Hendel explained that, in order to light a fire in a stable, one had to enter the building and pull down all the hay and the straw from the rack before laying the slow match on the floor. The slow match was then lit with a cigar, and the arsonist headed for home and was in bed before it went off. Hendel told Grove that coal oil was useless when it came to firing a building. Hendel had tried it himself when he set fire to Rheem's Hall, according to Grove's testimony.

Yet there was confusion among the prosecution's witnesses. Morrison testified how, in a different conversation, Hendel praised the use of coal oil as an accelerant. While maintaining his cover, Morrison told Hendel he did not see much use in burning down old buildings on the edge of Carlisle. He thought a fire downtown would have more of an impact. At that point, Hendel suggested torching a new church. "If coal oil was used, it would shine like a chandelier," Morrison said, quoting the bar owner. "It would go to heaven a-flying if a couple of gallons of coal oil were put on it."

Hendel then asked Morrison to buy him some coal oil for an upcoming fire. Morrison complied and testified how the accelerant was stored in the rear part of the saloon cellar. The prosecution then called James Lytle, who had shared a jail cell with Hendel after his arrest. A known criminal twice sentenced to state prison, Lytle was in the county lockup facing a charge of stealing a horse and buggy and serving out a sentence for stealing turkeys. Lytle overheard Hendel tell his bartender, Joe Thompson, to dispose of the bottle of coal oil stashed away in the cellar. Thompson denied this story on the witness stand. Witnesses for Hendel testified he was home or in his saloon when Rheem's Hall was set on fire. The jury found Hendel guilty.

Convicted of setting two fires, DeHuff received the most severe punishment of the five defendants. He was sentenced to ten years and nine months of hard labor at Eastern State Penitentiary in Philadelphia. State prison terms among the others varied. Widner received seven years and three months, while O'Donnell—the youngest, barely twenty-one years old—was sentenced to three years and six months. The court ordered Hendel confined for six years and nine months, while Grove would serve four years and six months for helping to convict the others. The *American*

Volunteer, in a January 18 article, summarized the public sentiment over the downfall of the firebugs:

> *These five young men have kept the citizens of Carlisle in constant dread, anxiety and terror for several years past. Prowling around town at all hours of the night with matches in one pocket and oil and cotton wick in another, they destroyed tens of thousands of dollars worth of property merely for the fun of the thing…Having long engaged in this infamous and wicked work, they became more bold and reckless…By dropping a word here and another there in unguarded moments, they invited the scrutiny of those who have been employed to ferret them out…*
>
> *It is not in our nature to rejoice over the prospective punishment of our fellow man but we do in common with all good citizens rejoice that* [those who] *have so long and so persistently harassed our people have at least been brought to trial and punishment…Of all bad men, the incendiary is the worst. His act is cowardly, unfeeling, devilish and malicious. Almost any man can find it in his heart to shoot down the incendiary in his tracks if caught in the act of firing a property just as you would shoot down a yellow mad dog. Every hand should be raised against the sneaking incendiary.*

Along with the venom, there was hope the defendants would use their time in prison to reflect on how alcohol use, together with idleness, caused their troubles. Seven years later, the *Sentinel* pushed to have John DeHuff released on parole after his father, Abram, died and left his aged mother without support. A printer by trade, John DeHuff used to work for the newspaper before his arrest on the arson charges. On January 19, 1884, the *Sentinel* published an editorial column written by an unnamed man who worked as a correspondent covering Tyrone for the *Altoona Call*. Below are some excerpts:

> *We played with him when he was a boy…We knew him in manhood and we speak the truth when we say that John DeHuff was only used as a cat's paw by others to burn the building…And at the time he was so drunk…he did not know what he was doing…Men were acquitted for murdering their fellow men when in this state, but young DeHuff for a much less offense of murder must have ten years of his life blighted, his hopes blasted and his health undermined.*

All this lobbying eventually helped. DeHuff was released after serving seven years in state prison and would be employed by the *Sentinel* for many years as a compositor setting type.

Closed Curtain

The Strand Theatre Arson

It seemed at first there was no escape for John Rhoades Jr. The twenty-year-old Carlisle man heard a loud thump before seeing the pall of dark smoke billow up from under his apartment door. Turning the knob to release the catch, he took a look outside and saw that flames in the third-floor hallway blocked his normal path out of the old Strand Theatre building. The survivor later testified that someone had piled an old chair, a portable television set and some rags in the exact same spot as the flames. He first saw the obstruction at about 2:35 a.m. the morning of August 29, 1972. Ten minutes later, Rhoades heard the noise, saw the fire and realized he was in a fight for his life.

Rhoades explained how he woke up Twila Failor, the woman he was living with at the time. In his panic, he pushed her out of the window, and she fell onto the sidewalk in front of the building at 11 North Pitt Street. Failor was hospitalized for eight days with a fractured ankle and broken ribs received while trying to escape, but she was lucky. Two other tenants died as a result of the fire, which spread and raged for three hours, resulting in a downtown disaster that closed four businesses and left at least fifteen people homeless.

Investigators found the severely burned body of twenty-six-year-old Steven Johnson amid the rubble of his third-floor apartment. A second victim, twenty-three-year-old Paula Wagner, died a day later in the intensive care unit of Harrisburg Hospital, where she was treated for injuries suffered after falling from a third-story window onto a parking meter. As for Rhoades, he jumped to safety onto the roof of what was then the Hamilton Library, now the headquarters of the Cumberland County Historical Society.

This 1972 photograph by James Steinmetz shows the ruins of the Strand Theatre building the morning of the fire.

At about 1:50 p.m. on August 29, Joseph Roebuck III, an orderly at Carlisle Hospital, noticed a woman exit a recovery room in a state of mild hysteria. Twenty-year-old Letitia Smallwood had just visited her old boyfriend, Richard Baltimore, who was drifting in and out of consciousness. He was being treated for a fractured wrist and facial burns suffered in the early morning fire. When Roebuck tried to comfort the woman, she blurted out, "You don't understand...You don't understand...It is because of me that the fire started." Jacqueline Bryson, a licensed practical nurse, testified that Smallwood was sobbing hysterically after she left Baltimore's hospital room. "It's my fault…It's my fault…I'm responsible for him being here," Bryson said, quoting Smallwood. When asked how she was responsible, Smallwood calmed down immediately but said nothing about starting the fire.

During her trial the following January, Smallwood took the stand in her own defense. She remembered telling Bryson, "It's my fault, because I wouldn't let him stay with me." Smallwood told jurors her statement at the hospital referred to an argument she and Baltimore had early in the evening of August 28 that prevented him from spending the night with her at the James Wilson Hotel, just down the street about half a block. Assistant District Attorney Edgar Bayley Jr. argued that Smallwood started the fire because she was romantically interested in Baltimore and upset that he lived with Paula Wagner, one of the victims.

Baltimore testified that he dated Smallwood while living with Wagner but that Wagner was his better half. He described a history of arguments between them that culminated in a veiled threat Smallwood made three days before the fire: "You'll be on the bottom, and I'll still be walking around." Rhoades testified that he saw Smallwood outside the apartment door of Wagner, his neighbor, at about 4:45 a.m. on August 28. Within minutes, he heard an argument coming from the direction of the apartment and one woman telling another, "I will get you, you b——." A short time later, Wagner was in critical condition at Harrisburg Hospital.

Smallwood told jurors she had no hard feelings toward Wagner and no thoughts of harming the couple. "I felt as though I was one of his women and he was one of my men," she said of Baltimore. Defense attorney Herbert Goldstein said Smallwood had many suitors and dated many people, so she wasn't only interested in Baltimore. He added Baltimore and Wagner also dated many people. Testimony revealed that Smallwood's family had filed assault charges against Baltimore on August 24, but these were dropped the next day. On the witness stand, Baltimore quoted Smallwood as saying, "I dropped the charges, but he still is messing around with Paula."

During the trial, Smallwood disputed eyewitness testimony she was at the Strand Theatre before, during and after the fire. Mary Jane Piffer, a tenant, told jurors she saw Smallwood on the street outside the building at about 9:00 p.m. on August 28, gesturing toward the third-floor apartment Wagner shares with Baltimore. Seven hours later, at about 4:00 a.m., August 29, Piffer saw the defendant sitting on the steps of a church across Pitt Street from the apartment building. Thomas Mazias, owner of the Hamilton Restaurant, testified he saw Smallwood enter his business at about 2:30 a.m. that morning to purchase either cigarettes or matches from a vending machine. The alarm for the Strand fire sounded at about 2:54 a.m.

The restaurant is located on the northeast corner of North Pitt and West High Streets, while the James Wilson Hotel (now the Safe Harbor homeless shelter) sits on the southwest corner of the same intersection. Smallwood testified she had no reason to visit the restaurant because she had purchased cigarettes earlier in the hotel lounge. She told jurors she was in bed asleep before 2:00 a.m. When called by the defense, bartender Marshall Washington corroborated the testimony that the defendant had been in the lounge buying cigarettes sometime before 2:00 a.m., but he also contradicted her story that she knew nothing about the false alarm that took place at about 1:58 a.m.

Firefighters had just returned to their homes when they were dispatched again at about 2:54 a.m. to the fire at the Strand. Crews from all five borough fire companies (Cumberland, Good Will, Union, Friendship and Empire) rushed to the scene, supported by units from Mount Holly Springs, Lower Allen Township and Camp Hill. Upon arrival, they saw flames rolling out of the windows and high into the night sky. The heat was intense. Witnesses saw several tenants jump from windows onto the sidewalk, while the *Sentinel* reported firemen rescuing six people using ladders. The fire gutted the second and third floors of the Strand Theatre, causing the roof and third floor to collapse. It was the final curtain for a historic downtown structure.

First opened in September 1898, the Strand Theatre was originally an L-shaped opera house with frontage on both North Pitt Street and Dickinson Avenue. The public entered through Pitt Street before taking a sharp turn to the left to enter the main hall, which was located in what is now the rear parking lot of the historical society. The hall seated 650 people on the floor, 550 more on the horseshoe-shaped balcony and another 200 in the gallery at the top. The building also housed a barbershop, billiards room and a bowling alley on the first floor, an assembly hall for banquets and dances on the second floor and third-floor meeting rooms, rented by four different Masonic lodges. The interior was heated by steam and illuminated by gas.

There was a packed house for its grand opening on September 1, 1898, that included delegations from every town in the Cumberland Valley to see a performance of John Philip Sousa's light opera *El Capitan*. In June 1904, faulty wiring caused a fire that destroyed the Masonic meeting rooms but spared the opera house. Four years later, management announced that films

This circa 1920 photograph shows the cast of a performance in the Carlisle Opera House in the Strand Theatre building.

would be shown every evening in the main hall or the second-floor assembly hall. The building operated primarily as a movie house until 1959. In 1925, it was renamed the Strand Theatre and served many years as the venue for Carlisle High School graduation ceremonies. At the time of the fire, the ground floor housed a private dwelling and army and air force recruiting stations while the upper floors had storage space and seven apartments.

After the disaster, firefighters cordoned off the area in front of the building because the façade was leaning forward and threatened to collapse. Untouched by the fire, the private dwelling and the recruiting stations were heavily damaged by water. Recruiters worked throughout the morning of August 29 to remove files and equipment for transfer to new offices as soon as such suitable facilities could be found and approved by the military.

Shifting through the rubble, State Police Fire Marshal William Sweet found no immediate cause of the fire. During the trial, Sweet failed to give specific facts to support his expert opinion that it was arson. In his closing statement to jurors, Goldstein argued insufficient evidence was presented to prove arson and that there was no testimony to suggest anyone, let alone his client, had started the fire.

As for Roebuck's testimony, Goldstein said it was possible the orderly misunderstood Smallwood. Three other witnesses present at the scene denied hearing her make the alleged confession outside her boyfriend's hospital room. With so much reasonable doubt, the verdict must be not guilty, Goldstein told the jury. But Bayley defended Roebuck as a man with an untarnished reputation. When Smallwood could not explain away Roebuck's testimony, she denied it, the prosecutor said. The jury deliberated for just over an hour on January 11, 1973, before finding Smallwood guilty of arson and two counts of first-degree murder. She was sentenced to life in state prison.

The building loss was estimated at over $100,000, about $515,000 in today's economy. Rather than repair the structure, owner Charles Kollas of Carlisle decided to demolish the building, so a crane was brought in on August 29 to knock down the façade. A month later, on September 27, the *Sentinel* reported how heavy debris on the second floor shifted, causing the north wall of the Strand to collapse onto the Hamilton Library next door. The impact left a hole about the size of a window in the museum and a three- by ten-foot gap in the library ceiling. While structural damage was estimated to be between $50,000 and $75,000, there was little or no damage to the contents of either the library or the museum. The historical society would later build an expansion on the lot formerly occupied by the Strand.

Twenty-seven years later, on December 18, 1999, a five-alarm fire swept through two downtown buildings located about half a block south of the historical society. The fire started just before 3:00 a.m. in the New York Deli at 48–50 West High Street before spreading west into the adjoining building. Close to two hundred firefighters from twenty-five agencies in the area battled the blaze for over three hours before it was brought under control. The fire left fifty-eight people homeless, caused an estimated $3 million in damage and destroyed five businesses and nine apartments.

Though investigators suspected arson, the case went unsolved for more than a year before authorities got a break while investigating a drug ring that included suspected crack cocaine dealing from an apartment above the deli. In November 2001, a federal jury convicted deli owner Arafat Maswadah of arson and related charges. Trial testimony revealed that the Carlisle businessman had hired three New York City men to burn his shop so he could collect $110,000 in insurance money. When these men were arrested on drug charges, they made plea bargains against Maswadah for lighter sentences. Maswadah was sentenced in June 2002 to thirty years in prison.

A crewman surveys the damage to the Cumberland County Historical Society following the collapse of the north wall of the Strand Theatre building into the museum and archive building.

This circa 1890 photograph shows the fire curtain at the Carlisle Opera House depicting Molly Pitcher at the Battle of Monmouth. It was painted by H.K. Diffendurfer.

Three months later, in September 2002, the county redevelopment authority entered into an agreement with 3T Investors to redevelop the West High Street property damaged in the December 1999 arson. The $1.36 million project transformed the Centenary building and a vacant lot near the corner of West High and South Pitt Streets into a building featuring first-floor retail slots and upscale second-floor apartments. The Centenary building was originally a church built in 1876.

Bibliography

PART I. FRONTIER FELONS

Temple of Fame: The Plight of Christopher Shockey

American Volunteer. "A Record of Crimes: History of Murder in Cumberland County." December 23, 1869.

Conrad, W.P. *From Terror to Freedom in the Cumberland Valley.* Greencastle, PA: Lillian F. Beshore Memorial Library, 1976.

McClellan, John Howard. "Colonial Counterfeiters of the Blue Ridge." Paper presented before the Kittochtinny Historical Society, Chambersburg, PA, November 17, 1988.

Wing, Rev. Conway. *History of Cumberland County.* Philadelphia, PA: Herald Printing, 1979.

My Manifold Crimes: Lewis the Robber

American Volunteer. Untitled column on attempted robbery. April 27, 1820.

Barrick, Mac E. "Lewis the Robber in Life and Legend." *Pennsylvania Folklore* (August 1967).

Evening Sentinel. "Lewis the Robber." April 29, 1898.

———. "Lewis the Robber." May 6, 1898.

———. "Lewis the Robber." May 19, 1898.

Fisher, Forest K. "Pennsylvania's Robin Hood: David 'Robber' Lewis Stalked the Juniata Valley." *Notes from Monument Square*, newsletter published by Mifflin County Historical Society. (March, April and May 2006).

Franz, Linda. "Outlaw with a Conscience." *Sentinel*, March 7, 2004.

Hepford, David. "Lewis the Robber." *Harrisburg Telegraph*, November 28, 1938.

Hoch, Paul D. *Carlisle History and Lore: Its People, Places and Stories*. Carlisle, PA: Cumberland County Historical Society, 2003.

Rishel, C.D. *The Life and Adventures of David Lewis: The Robber and Counterfeiter*. Newville, PA: C.D. Rishel, printed by editor, n.d.

Wing, Conway. *History of Cumberland County*. Philadelphia, PA: Herald Printing, 1979.

PART II. CRUEL DAYS

A Passion to Tatters: Town-Gown Troubles

American Volunteer. "The Affair at the College Again." May 18, 1843.

———. "Blackguardism." May 4, 1843.

———. "Polite Literature." May 25, 1843.

Carlisle Herald. "Fire and Fight." November 1, 1888.

Carlisle Herald & Expositor. "A Disclaimer." May 10, 1843.

———. "A Hoax." May 24, 1843.

———. "That College Affair." May 24, 1843.

Evening Sentinel. "The Burgess Has Something to Say..." November 3, 1888.

———. "Fracas Between Town and Students." November 1, 1888.

———. "A Student's Opinion..." November 2, 1888.

———. "The Student's Side." November 2, 1888.

Sellers, Charles Coleman. *Dickinson College: A History*. Middletown, CT: Wesleyan University Press, 1973.

Impulse of the Moment: Nasty College Pranks

Hoch, Paul D. *Carlisle History and Lore: Its People, Places and Stories*. Carlisle, PA: Cumberland County Historical Society, 2003.

King, Horatio Collins. "Journal of My College Life." Publisher unknown.

Morgan, James Henry. *Dickinson College, The History of 150 Years 1783–1933*. Carlisle, PA: Dickinson College, 1933.

New York Times. "College Prank Played on the President of Dickinson College." January 22, 1875.

Sellers, Charles Coleman. *Dickinson College: A History.* Middletown, CT: Wesleyan University Press, 1973.

False Fabric...Liquor Evil: Indian School Woes

Adams County News. "Clean Slate for Moses Friedman." October 23, 1915.

———. "Employees Did Not Testify." March 28, 1914.

———. "Friedman Says No Charges Yet." February 21, 1914.

———. "Friedman Wants Investigation." July 11, 1914.

———. "Hear Testimony." May 15, 1915.

———. "Indian School Difficulties Will Be Followed Up." December 19, 1914.

———. "Indian School Troubles Again." January 31, 1914.

———. "More Trouble at Carlisle School." May 2, 1914.

———. "Nori Has Also Been Suspended." April 4, 1914.

———. "Say They Burned Public Records." January 16, 1915.

———. "Will Not Move Indian School." February 7, 1914.

Bell, Genevieve. "Telling Stories Out of School: Remembering the Carlisle Indian Industrial School 1879–1918." Graduate dissertation, Department of Anthropology and the Committee on Graduate Studies, Stanford University, June 1998.

Carlisle Herald. "19-Year-Old Hazel Myers Was Murdered..." May 24, 1914.

"Carlisle Indian School." Transcript of Hearings before the Joint Commission of Congress. Government Printing Office, Washington, D.C. 1914. This includes the inspection report by Linnen quoted in the text.

Cress, Joseph. *Remembering Carlisle: Tales from the Cumberland Valley.* Charleston, SC: The History Press, 2010.

Evening Sentinel. "Conditions for Indians Better Without License." January 14, 1915.

———. "Denies Nori Confession." March 30, 1914.

———. "Friedman and Nori Indicted." January 15, 1915.

———. "Friedman Suspended." February 13, 1914.

———. "Inspector's Report Concerns Warner." May 26, 1914.

———. "Investigation Adjourned." February 9, 1914.

———. "No Developments in Murder Case." May 26, 1914.

———. "The Nori Hearing." March 25, 1914.

———. "Nothing New in Murder Case." May 27, 1914.

———. "Petition of Students Caused Investigation." February 7, 1914.

———. Untitled pro-Warner editorial. May 25, 1914.

———. "Whole Story Laid Bare." May 28, 1914.

Gettysburg Times. "Irregularities at Indian School." February 10, 1914.

———. "New Sensation." March 30, 1914.

———. "Probers Visits Indian School." February 7, 1914.

———. "Suspend School Superintendent." February 13, 1914.

Hilton, John. "'Pop' Warner Devised Grid Innovations." *Sentinel*, February 27, 2000.

Star and Sentinel (Gettysburg). "Carlisle Superintendent Order to Return to Post." January 31, 1914.

———. "Friedman Blames Politics." June 13, 1914.

———. "Friedman Goes Free." June 19, 1914.

———. "Indian School Head May Not Be Prosecuted." July 11, 1914.

———. "Lipps Made Head of Carlisle School." May 15, 1915.

———. "Will Not Be Tried in Cumberland County." November 14, 1914.

Witmer, Linda F. *The Indian Industrial School: Carlisle, Pennsylvania 1879–1918.* Carlisle, PA: Cumberland County Historical Society, 1993.

PART III. LURID LEGENDS

Hanger-On: Rowdy Old Schimmel

American Volunteer. "Assault." May 13, 1869.

Blymire, David. "Colorful Folk Art Returns to Cumberland County." *Sentinel*, February 11, 2002.

Carlisle Herald. "A Bold Piece of Work." May 14, 1869.

———. "A False Alarm." March 6, 1879.

———. "Schimmel Dead." August 7, 1890.

Carlisle Herald & Mirror. "A Narrow Escape from Death." May 25, 1883.

Daily Evening Sentinel. "A Genuine Duel." August 2, 1883.

———. "Old John Schimmel." February 15, 1883.

———. "Old Schimmel." May 24, 1887.

Evening Sentinel. "Schimmel Dead." August 7, 1890.

Hoch, Paul. "Old Schimmel." *Early American Life* (February 1977).

Lindt, Susan. "Art Collectors: Schimmel True Original." *Sentinel*, February 27, 2000.

Pass, Karl H. "Wilhelm Schimmel: Cumberland County 'Image Maker' (1817–1890)." *Cumberland County History* (Winter 2002).

A Warm Reception: The Jack the Hugger Affair

Evening Sentinel. "Another Jack the Hugger." October 23, 1924.
———. "Jack the Hugger." March 31, 1917.
———. "Police Arrest Jack the Hugger." October 12, 1925.
Logan Journal. "How Many Jacks?" October 18, 1890.

Moral Plague Spot: The House of Cora

Ancestry.com. 1860 United States Federal Census.
Cress, Joseph. *Murder & Mayhem in Cumberland County.* Charleston, SC: The History Press, 2010.
Evening Sentinel. "Andrews Woman Gets 13 Months." May 19, 1923.
———. "Andrews Woman Is Found Guilty." May 15, 1923.
———. "Bawdy House Is Raided." November 5, 1917.
———. "Carlisle Indians Present." May 2, 1911.
———. "Cora Andrews Found Guilty." May 3, 1911.
———. "First Case Tried." May 14, 1923.
Garner, Bryan A. *Black's Law Dictionary, Seventh Edition.* St. Paul, MN: West Group, 1999.
Zdinak, Paul. *Bessie's House.* Harrisburg, PA: Your Private Printer, 1976.

A Carlisle Institution: Madam Bessie Jones

Beers, Paul. "Reporter at Large." *Patriot*, n.d.
Brann, James W. "Area Woman Held on Evading Tax On $86,000." *Patriot*, May 3, 1961.
Cress, Joseph. *Murder & Mayhem in Cumberland County.* Charleston, SC: The History Press, 2010.
Evening Sentinel. "Bessie Jones House Robbed by Six Gunmen." May 20, 1972.
———. "Burglary Probe Here Continues." January 22, 1964.
———. "Carlisle Woman Is Sentenced." July 12, 1961.

——. "County Court Sentences 9." April 28, 1959.

——. "Fourth Person Held in Fire Burglary." January 21, 1964.

——. "Sentence Court Conducted Here." September 20, 1963.

——. "Seven Arrested Liquor Seized in Carlisle Raid." May 10, 1941.

——. "3 Women Held in Raid Here." June 20, 1963.

——. "Trio in Raid Held for Trial." April 14, 1959.

——. "2 Accused of Trying to Rob Bessie's House." May 4, 1972.

——. "U.S. in Hunt for Owners of Money." January 24, 1964.

——. "Woman Faces Arson Charge." January 20, 1964.

——. "Woman Faces Tax Charges." May 3, 1961.

Harrisburg Evening News. "Woman Accused of Tax Evasion." May 3, 1961.

Smith, Robert Detective Sergeant. Arrest report found in court papers pertaining to case of *Commonwealth v. Bessie Jones*, docket number 105, September 1963.

——. Arrest report found in court papers pertaining to case of *Commonwealth v. Bessie Jones*, docket number 141, September 1968.

Witmer, Linda F. "Hyman Goldstein." In *Cumberland Justice: Legal Practice in Cumberland County, 1750 to 2000.* Carlisle, PA: Cumberland County Bar Foundation, 2001.

Zdinak, Paul. *Bessie's House.* Harrisburg, PA: Your Private Printer, 1976.

PART IV. DEVILISH DOINGS

Issue of Identity: The Extradition of Albert Hazlett

American Volunteer. "Arrest of a Man Supposed to Be Captain Cook." October 27, 1859.

——. "Conviction of Hazlett." February 16, 1860.

——. "Execution of Hazlett and Stephens." March 22, 1860.

——. "The Supposed Insurgent in Our Jail." November 3, 1859.

——. "Taken to Virginia for Trial." November 10, 1859.

Anderson, Osborne. *A Voice from Harper's Ferry.* Boston, 1861.

Carlisle American. "Arrest of a Supposed Harpers Ferry Insurrectionist." October 26, 1859.

——. "Communicated Carlisle." November 9, 1859.

——. "Hazlett and Stephens." February 22, 1860.

——. "Hearing of the Harpers Ferry Insurgent." November 9, 1859.

——. "Hearing on Saturday." November 2, 1859.

Carlisle Herald. "The Harpers Ferry Fugitive." November 2, 1859.

———. "The Harpers Ferry Fugitive." November 9, 1859.

Cress, Joseph. "Cumberland County's Connection to John Brown's Raid at Harpers Ferry." *Cumberland County History* 26 (2009): 48–60.

"One of John Brown's Raiders." *200 Years in Cumberland County.* Carlisle, PA: The Hamilton Library and Historical Association, 1851. Reprinted from W.J. Shearer. "John Brown's Raid." Hamilton Library, 1905.

Shippensburg News. "Carlisle Ink Drops." November 12, 1859.

———. "William Harrison." November 5, 1859.

Thompson, D.W. *Carlisle Outlaw: The Life and Times of Charley Foulk 1837 to 1884.* Carlisle, PA: Thompson's Book Store, 1975.

Wassel, Marcia, Interview by Joseph David Cress, October 2004.

Infernal Machine: The Story of Charley Foulk

American Volunteer. "An Infernal Machine." February 3, 1876.

———. "Court Proceedings." April 20, 1876.

Carlisle Herald. "Court Proceedings." April 20, 1876.

Carlisle Mirror. "The Dynamite Fiends' Second Operation." March 31, 1876.

———. "A Fiendish Act." February 1, 1876.

Cress, Joseph. *Murder & Mayhem in Cumberland County.* Charleston, SC: The History Press, 2010.

Fralish, John C., Jr. *Carlisle Public Graveyard Index and Map.* Carlisle, PA. n.d.

Hoch, Paul D. *Carlisle History and Lore: Its People, Places and Stories.* Carlisle, PA: Cumberland County Historical Society, 2003.

Thompson, D.W. *Carlisle Outlaw: The Life and Times of Charley Foulk, 1837–1884.* Carlisle, PA: Thompson's Bookstore, 1975.

Valley Sentinel. "Another Fearful Explosion." March 31, 1876.

———. "What Next?" January 28, 1876.

Fire Fiends: An Arson Ring Broken

American Volunteer. "January Court." January 11, 1877.

———. "January Court." January 18, 1877.

———. "More Incendiarism." November 23, 1876.

———. "Trial, Conviction and Sentence of the Incendiaries." January 18, 1877.

Carlisle Herald. "Fire Fiends." November 2, 1876.

———. "January Court." January 11, 1877.

———. "January Court." January 18, 1877.

Carlisle Mirror. "Court Proceedings." January 16, 1877.

———. "The Incendiary." November 21, 1876.

Hoch, Paul. *Carlisle History and Lore: Its People, Places and Stories.* Carlisle, PA: Cumberland County Historical Society, 2003.

"Night of the Tannery Fire 1876." *Two Hundred Years in Cumberland County.* Carlisle, PA: Hamilton Library and Historical Association, 1951. Reprinted from the *American Volunteer,* January 18, 1877.

"Postscript 1884." *Two Hundred Years in Cumberland County.* Carlisle, PA: Hamilton Library and Historical Association, 1951. Reprinted from the *Daily Evening Sentinel,* January 19, 1884.

"Take Back Your New Fangled Engines." *Two Hundred Years in Cumberland County.* Carlisle, PA: Hamilton Library and Historical Association, 1951. Reprinted from the *American Volunteer,* November 30, 1876.

Thompson, Allen D. "The Sentinel As It Was." A column published in the *Sentinel,* n.d.

Thompson, D.W. *Carlisle Outlaw: The Life and Times of Charley Foulk, 1837–1884.* Carlisle, PA: Thompson's Bookstore, 1975.

Valley Sentinel. "And Still Another." November 24, 1876.

Closed Curtain: The Strand Theatre Arson

Evening Sentinel. "Fire Loss Put at $100,000." August 30, 1972.

———. "Girl Charged with Murder." September 5, 1972.

———. "New Trial Sought in Fire Case." January 20, 1973.

———. "Threat Bared in Murder-Arson Trial Testimony." January 10, 1973.

———. "Woman 2d Victim of Fire." August 31, 1972.

Garrett, Clarke. *In Pursuit of Pleasure: Leisure in Nineteenth Century Cumberland County.* Carlisle, PA: Cumberland County Historical Society, 1997.

Hilton, John. "Investors Take Over Centenary Building." *Sentinel,* September 14, 2002.

———. "Jury: Owner Guilty of Arson Threats." *Sentinel,* November 27, 2001.

———. "Maswadah Gets 30 Years In 1999 Arson." *Sentinel,* June 5, 2002.

———. "1 Year Later, Fire Still Mystery." *Sentinel,* December 18, 2000.

Jones, Ray. "Girl Held for Court in Deaths." *Evening Sentinel*, September 22, 1972.

Jones, Ray, and Leslie Trout. "Fire at Strand Theater Building Kills 1." *Evening Sentinel*, August 29, 1972.

Kahn, Harold. "Defense Rests Case in Murder Trial." *Evening Sentinel*, January 11, 1973.

————. "Jury Declares First Degree Murder Charges." *Evening Sentinel*, January 12, 1973.

————. "Testimony Heard in Murder Trial." *Evening Sentinel*, January 9, 1973.

Trout, Leslie. "Wall Cave-In Damages Hamilton Library." *Evening Sentinel*, September 27, 1972.

About the Author

Joseph David Cress is an award-winning journalist with twenty-one years of full-time newspaper experience. He has worked as a staff reporter with the *Sentinel* in Carlisle for thirteen years. *Wicked Carlisle* is his fourth book with The History Press. Prior works include *Remembering Carlisle: Tales from the Cumberland Valley*, *Murder & Mayhem in Cumberland County* and *Murder & Mayhem in York County*. Cress lives in York, Pennsylvania, with his wife Stacey, dogs Patches and Rosco and tomcats Chewie and Boone.